Where East Eats West

The Street-Smarts Guide
To Business in China

SAM GOODMAN

First Printed August 2009
Revised Edition November 2011

Published by Create Publishing
A division of Amazon
7290 B. Investment Drive
Charleston, South Carolina
www.booksurge.com
BUS025000   BUSINESS & ECONOMICS/Entrepreneurship

ISBN-10: 1-4392-2830-2
ISBN-13: 978-1-439-22830-2

This book is dedicated to my life's two "Sigs":

My father - Sigmund Goodman
My role model who motivated me to always strive to be the best I can be.

&

My daughter - Sophie Yang Goodman (S.Y.G)
Who is my sunshine and motivates me to be the best dad I can be.

Acknowledgements

Like most accomplishments in my life, I cannot say I got here entirely on my own. Without the motivation, help and guidance from a number of other people this book would never have been finished. To give any indication of this, I started putting thoughts for this book down in 2003.

I would never have finished this book were it not for two women: my wife Lea, who got me off my butt to get this going and my co-author, Michelle Ree who was the writing glue who kept the whole project together. Michelle made the entire book writing process easy for me. Basically I talked a lot to start and did some sculpting at the end. She is responsible for the best grammatically written parts of the book.

I also would like to thank David Wolf, the grosse mensch, whose guidance, encouragement and insight was invaluable throughout the editing and finalizing of the book. Eric Abrahamsen, master editor; my hat is tipped to you and to Brenda, from the pear tree company, for your patience and excellent formatting of all the formats. And finally thank you to my eldest sister Jennifer Goodman, who also provided insight and editing and, by the time she finishes editing everything, we should be ready for the next edition.

Table of Contents

Setting Yourself Up To Succeed
   Being Able To Dress Yourself and Tie Your Own Shoes

Dealing With The Government

Just imagine something witty about lying down with snakes or swimming with sharks or rolling around in manure… the odds are you are not going to come out of the experience unscathed

Mega Markets

Holy Crap Batman! Look at All Those People!........

Quick bit by the author

Wow… It has been over 2 years since this little book for entrepreneurs has come out and no one was surprised more than me when university after university started picking it up and using it in their curriculum.

I've had the pleasure to visit and lecture internationally, do the whole radio and a bit of tv thing. The message is always the same; this is called Where East Eats West not because China is out to cheat you, but because the typical Westerner comes to China uninformed and unprepared on how the 'rules' of doing business are interpreted differently and gets eaten alive.

Bottom line, the 'Us' vs 'Them' attitude is bogus. Everything that happens in China does in fact, happen everywhere else; it's just a matter of degree. Using an I.C.U. (I see you) process, Identifying the issue, Connecting it to things you already know and Understanding the difference. You quickly realize (illegal actions aside) most 'problems' are little more than a shift to the right or to the left on that 1-10 scale of how often this happens..

Your attitude towards and understanding of China, going in, is going to greatly affect your chances of not getting eaten alive.

Yes, China has changed tremendously. You leave for two weeks and come back to find old buildings gone and new skyscrapers in their place. It will astound you and boggles the mind when you compare it to the relative snail's pace of development in North America and in Europe.

That said, human nature does not change that fast.; Westerners still come to China with the same misconceptions, make the same mistakes and while the Chinese used to want bikes, now they want BMWs.

Ok, Ok... Chinese born after 1980 **do** think very differently and in twenty to thirty years when they are running things, I'm sure China will be a very different place. Until then, I'm still willing to bet you three hours of your time that by reading this book, you will benefit greatly

If you are new to China, I hope you enjoy the read and laugh as much as you learn.

If you are not new to China, I hope you enjoy the read and can laugh at all the shared ~~mistakes~~ experiences

Cheers
Sam Goodman
11/11/18

Section I

Introduction

Which would you prefer: getting roughed up by someone who cares or getting the crap kicked out of you by someone who doesn't?

1. CHINA FEVER

It wasn't too long ago that internet fever made a hefty percentage of the best and brightest in the West delirious with ambition and greed. The internet boomed for a few years at the turn of the millennium and then crashed in a matter of months. Millions made by entrepreneurs barely old enough to drink were lost before they had time to blow them the old-fashioned way: through bad marriages, worse divorces and lawyering-slash-rehab for their spoiled, delinquent children.

Right now, parts of the Western world are being swept by a new fever, one just as intoxicating: China fever. It's characterized by the recurring dream of selling **just one** widget to the over 1 BILLION Chinese.

Tale of the Tape			
	US	**Europe**	**China**
Size	3,794,066 mi²	3,930,000 mi²	3,704,427 mi²
	9,826,630 km²	10,180,000 km²	9,671,018 km²
Population	305,746,000	731,000,001	1,321,851,888
Cities with > 1 million people	9	36	~100

All found from a Wiki search

Yes, the dragon has certainly awakened. It's big, it's tough, it's glittering and to many, it's enticing. China is roaring to life economically, is the manufacturing center of the world and it's the place to be - no, HAVE to be, if you want to make money.

But be warned: It will warm, toast and then slow-roast you before you know what's happening. And then it will eat you up, like it has so many others who have gone before you. That is, if you don't come to the fight armed and you stay alert... if you become delirious with China Fever.

2. THE GOAL OF THIS BOOK

This book, *Where East Eats West*, is designed to offer those delirious with 'China fever' a few extra-strength aspirin, to help them ice themselves down and snap the hell out of it before they screw up their lives and their fortunes irreparably.

The Goal of this book:

Accelerate your China learning curve to help you accomplish your goals;
AKA Skip making elementary China business mistakes so you can get right into making advanced ones. [*]

In these pages, I've purposefully painted a rough and tough picture of the Chinese business environment, because it *is* rough and tough – and because I'd rather you find yourself pleasantly surprised when things go smoothly than caught unaware by a sucker punch.

Please Note: *Where East Eats West* is **not** an analytical look at the business climate of the fastest-growing economy in the world. It is not a corporate etiquette guide or a comprehensive how-to book on doing business in China. Plenty of those have already been

---

[*] If I can also decrease the overall understanding gap the West has regarding China well, that would be swell too.

written – and then some. Instead, it's an on-the-ground, in-the-trenches, street-smarts guide of lessons that entrepreneurs in China have learned the hard way.

It's designed to give people, especially entrepreneurs who are thinking about doing business in mainland China a heads-up about some of the red-hot realities that are going to give them big, burning bites in the behind when they least expect it.

It's designed to help *you* think more deeply about your decision to stake your future and your fortunes on this wild, exciting place. And it's designed to prepare you to survive the thrashings ahead, when you decide to go for it, anyway.

And, on a very practical level, it's designed to accelerate your China business education - to help you avoid making elementary China business mistakes so you can get right to making advanced ones.

It's the book I wish I could have bought 13 years ago, when I started my own enterprise in China.

Oh… yeah. Let's just get another thing clear, I am by no means a Sinophile (someone who loves thinking about and expounding on all things Chinese).

Nor am I an academic. (All of my high school teachers would attest to this, I have no doubt. I am sure my university professors would as well, if they could remember me.) What I am is a guy who has been there, seen it, done that, and lived to tell the tale. And if you're smart, you'll listen and learn. You've heard the saying, "A penny saved is a penny earned." Well, this book could save you lots of pennies – millions, in fact.

3. THIS BOOK IS FOR YOU IF...

- You or your spouse are gutsy entrepreneurs and are thinking about pulling up stakes and heading across the ocean in search of fortune, fame and smoking good stories you can tell your grandkids.

- You have received the corporate memo that you are about to be transplanted to China for the "OPPORTUNITY OF A LIFETIME," to head up the country operations and well, you are scared witless. Relax. You're on the right track. You're reading this.

- You are already in China trying to do some good business and struggling to maintain your faith in your own vision (and the essential goodness of humankind).

- You have been doing business in China for a long time (three years or more) and simply need a good laugh and know that you are not alone.

Of course, this book may be a waste of your money if...

You are one of those rare geniuses who have no need to learn from others. You will break the mold, carve new ground, and prove that those who came (and fizzled) before you were lesser beings whose outcomes would have been entirely different had they possessed your intellect, business savvy and all-around cross-cultural prowess.

No, you are not the first person with those thoughts and no, you will not be the last. I laugh so hard milk comes out my nose every time I hear a Westerner tell me they've "got it covered" because they've "done a lot of business with Asian people" or "have been in business for 25 years." But seriously, don't let your past experiences or successes lull you into complacency. Pay attention to the information you're about to read in this book.

Don't get me wrong - there are other ways to get this information. But there certainly isn't an *easier* way. Lawyers and consultants will gladly take hundreds of dollars per hour to wax poetic, telling you a lot of the same stuff. They will however use more biz school lingo.

So grab a snack or a beer, get comfortable and get ready for the straight truth on all the ways you can screw up doing business in China.

4. BOTTOM LINE –
What are we dealing with here?

The China market will probably eat you alive.

China certainly welcomes your money, your knowledge, your experience, your technology, pretty much anything you have that they don't.

BUT!!!... Don't think that it is *you* who are entirely welcomed.

You are often seen as a tool.

And like a tool, you will be used when needed and then cast aside.
DEAL WITH IT.

We are talking about the wild, Wild West in the EAST.
You are in their house, trying to make money off of them. You think they don't know that? Come on, Mainland Chinese are extremely pragmatic. They *wants* some of what you *gots* and they're willing to do just about anything to get it.

Generally speaking....
In the West, people are taught to believe that the ends do NOT justify the means. Here, however, the law of the jungle kicks in and the ends do in fact tend to justify the

means. Lying, cheating and stealing is not something people openly support here, but when you get right down to it, if it gets them where they want to go then ....

And don't forget... as you are not one of "them," which makes doing it that much easier; given the ingrained belief that foreigners have screwed over China so many times, you now owe them.

No, not everyone is like this, but you will be shocked at the number of people who are.

Don't forget, China is still a develop-PING nation and with such a huge population, think "jungle mentality." (China in Chinese is pronounced "Zhong Guo," which sounds a bit like Jun-gle.)

Here is my version of the disclaimer.
I am not a lawyer. Nor should any of the following information be considered a substitute for legal advice.

On the one side, there are too many lawyers out there who are focused on covering their own asses and give "so-cautious-you-have-no-room-to-move" advice. On the flip side there are a handful of lawyers who have been in China a long time and seen so many deals that they know when you are on the road that leads to a cliff.

By the end of this book you should be able to brush past the basics (saving you a few hundred bucks right there) and have enough understanding of the environment to NOT choose the first lawyer you come across NOR expect to use the same lawyer you have been using at home.

5. THE ANTI ANTI-CHINA RANT

OK, enough of the China bashing and enough of the China horror stories. Yes, bashing China is easy to do. (Bashing of any kind usually is.)

Bashing a culture that does not represent your values or beliefs is always easy to do. And, it's always a mistake. Sure, there are a number of things that go on in this country that I don't agree with, and not all of them have to do with the business environment. But no country is perfect and I guarantee you that an outsider looking in on your country or mine could and would find plenty to criticize.

I hate the pollution that clouds the skies of Beijing, my adopted home city. It sucks. On the bad days, I grumble. On the good days, I smile. It's the same in business.

So "the China price" is kicking your butt? So your customers aren't loyal to your product? So your suppliers are having you for dinner – and not as a guest? So your competitors copied your product design, and they're manufacturing and selling your product for 30% less than you?

You're right. It's rough. It's tough. It's not fair. It's not right. What can you do?

Innovate or die.

Find new ways to improve and promote your product or service. Get a new product or service. Get a new attitude. Or get out of business. But don't get caught in the trap that snares so many Western entrepreneurs in China and waste your time and energy complaining about the realities of doing business here. Don't bitch and moan about the system, the bureaucracy, the lack of respect for intellectual property, or the crazy zoning laws. Don't even hope or work for better conditions. Get creative and work with the way things are now.

Invest the energy generated by your frustration in finding smart solutions to the problems that face you today, one by one by one. And if it's time for you to pack up and go home, do it knowing you gave it your best shot, and you've learned a lot about business, China, people, and perseverance. You'll find a way to leverage what you've learned into financial and life resources that will make your investment pay dividends – regardless of how your China enterprise ends.

As low as China can take you – that's how high it will allow you to soar. The challenges are immense, matched only by the opportunities. As it was in America's Old West, there are fortunes being made in China that couldn't be made anywhere else in the world. There are also experiences to be had and friendships to be built that can make you a richer, better person than you thought you could be - if you're ready for them.

Read on and keep your eye on the prize. China is a magical, mystifying, messy land where victory is hard won, which makes it so very, very sweet.

6. GETTING STARTED

There is no business school, no corporate internship, no real-life-in-the-trenches entrepreneurial experiences in the West that can <u>fully</u> prepare you for starting a business in China.

So, what can you do if you want to start a business in China and you have no China business experience?

1. You can "go corporate." You can take a job in China chopping wood and carrying water for a company that's doing something a lot like what you want to do. While there, you can learn as much as possible, and then go out and apply what you've learned to your own business.

2. You can just *go*. You can pull up stakes, head on over to the Middle Kingdom, "learn by doing" (a.k.a. "The School of Hard Knocks") and let the chips fall where they may.

3. You can get mentored. You can read books, hire consultants, search out advisors, and otherwise make use of wisdom gleaned through other entrepreneurs' experiences.

I suggest you do Option #1 or do it in combination with Option #3. It worked for Kung Fu, and it will work for you.

By itself, Option #1 – "going corporate" for awhile, has intensive time requirements, means postponing your dream, and has obvious limitations. I mean, by the time you've gotten enough experience under your belt to make a real difference, your dream may have died. It may no longer have a market – or that market may have been filled. And frankly, there's a lot you can't learn about entrepreneurship in the corporate world. (I'm assuming you are not going in as the operations side of someone else's company. Because who the hell would hire a non China experienced manager...right?)

By itself, Option #2 – "learning as you go" is the toughest – and most likely to leave you penniless. I'm sorry to say that it's also the option of choice for most Western entrepreneurs on the Mainland. Sure, the School of Hard Knocks is generally considered a peerless educational institution, but by the time you master half of the courses it offers, you'll be on your way home, tail between your legs. Whipped.

A combination with Option #3 is the thinking person's option. Learn, learn, learn from others' mistakes, successes and insights. You can do that by paying attention to what you read in this book, checking out the *Recommended Resources* at the back, joining the community at **<u>WhereEastEatsWest.com</u>**, and by calling up people who've been there and done that, and asking for their advice.

Grasshopper, go to China on fire to succeed, but don't go expecting to succeed instantly. Attachment to specific outcomes (like actually making money) will only set you up to be plagued by fear and anxiety when things don't seem to be going your way – which will probably be the case most of the time.

(Sound of a gong....)

7. OK, WHO IS SAM GOODMAN ANYHOW?

Born October 28, 1971, in Toronto.
That makes me a Scorpio and a Pig, Year of the Pig that is.
I am Canadian.

I had a great childhood.
My Mom was a great mom (still is). Awesome cook and a great baker too.
My dad worked hard and played hard. He had a sense of humor and a solid work ethic; great combination.

I have two older sisters. Jen's the eldest, 5 years older. She and I take after my old man, we're both into sports. So in many respects growing up was like having an older brother, because when I was really little, she used to beat me up which in hindsight is probably partially responsible for toughening me up. (Um…Thanks Jen)

The middle child, Becky, was the "princess." She seemed to never get in trouble; I got into lots. She had her benefits, but they only blossomed after we moved to Texas; first Dallas and then Plano.

I loved growing up in Texas. I had great friends, the weather was awesome and did lots of playing outdoors.

Becky was a cheerleader for five years and because we had a big front yard, the cheerleading squad used to come over to our house to practice. (Thank you Becky)

I started my first business when I was eleven. I even had cards printed:

Goodman is the Best Man
For lawn mowing, fence painting, and babysitting

I made enough money cutting lawns that summer to buy myself a BMX bike. I liked earning my own money. My mom was definitely the greatest help. I wasn't strong enough to lift the lawnmower into the car trunk, so my mom used to drive me to my jobs at like 7 mph, while I sat in the trunk, holding the lawnmower, dragging it the whole way. (Thank you Mom)

When I was 14, I weighed about 88 lbs, I started wrestling and won Texas State champ. For that I have my dad to thank. You see, he wouldn't let me compete unless I was in proper shape so, in addition to wrestling practice he used to make me run every day. When I won that final match, he was so happy, he picked me up in a bear hug, screaming and cheering. I swear he was happier than I was.

Shortly thereafter, I left Texas to return to Toronto to go to a boarding school. Man, that whole thing took me by surprise.

I think I was 12 when my dad went to Toronto on a business trip and asked if I wanted to join. I thought, "Sure, I can see some of my old friends and my cousins." During a car ride, we passed by the grounds of Upper Canada College (UCC). Founded in 1829, UCC is Canada's top boys school and possesses some prime real estate in Toronto. As we passed by, my dad nonchalantly asked if I would be interested in going to a school like that.

Without thinking anything of it, I said, "Yeah. Sure." He said he'd look into it...

A few months later he asked if I wanted to go for an interview. "Sure." Go see my old friends and play with my cousins again. No brainer. I went. I saw. May have even said a "Yes sir," once or twice and that was it.

The end of grade nine was rolling near and I got called to the principal's office. I was 14 and although I did well in school, I was certainly no angel. My brain was spinning, wondering what I had done or what they found out about.

I arrive, and there are my dad and my mom, with balloons... I was accepted to UCC.

Oh jeez.

High school is an important part of a kid's life. My sister was a cheerleader. I was a wrestling star (OK. 88 lbs... a very small star). Puberty was going to arrive any second now and I was going to be shipped off to Canada to go to an all-boys boarding school?

Not exactly the high school experience I expected...

Well, to make a long story short, UCC was great. Not because I had nothing but fun but because it whipped me into academic shape and yeah, I had loads of fun while I was there too.

Unfortunately, right before I graduated high school, my dad died. He was 55, I was 17. He had a heart attack. Boom. He was gone.

The next year or so was a blur. I finished high school, I worked three jobs that summer (Not because I needed the money, but to keep me occupied. My college was paid for by family and friends of my father. They all chipped in some money to take care of me and my sister's education. Talk about good friends... and I vaguely remember picking my first year university courses on my own.

I went to the University of Western Ontario (UWO). It was nice enough. I just couldn't wait to get it over and done with. The greatest thing about my UWO time was the friends I made. But just about as soon as I graduated, I moved to Hong Kong.

Why?

Well in addition to wrestling, I took martial arts growing up, loved watching Black Belt Theater as a kid (*The Man with the Golden Arm, The Seven Deadly Swords*...awesome stuff), studied Oriental Philosophy in university and well, think that Asian women are just gorgeous.

I knew one guy living in Hong Kong and no one in Japan.

So, with no plan and very little money, I moved to Hong Kong. I slept on my buddy's couch for a month. I had no idea what I wanted to do and after graduating with a BA in Psychology. I had no marketable skills.

So what does a fit kid do in Hong Kong? Well, I studied...to be a fitness instructor. I took two international courses, got certified and poof, I was a fitness instructor.

It was great. I worked about three hours a day and got paid as much as my buddy, the architect, who worked nine hours a day. By the end of my stint in Hong Kong, at the ripe old age of 22, I was managing the Health Club at the Sheraton. Seriously... No kidding. I was managing the whole health club at 22.

It might sound cool, but it didn't work out very well. I had to give up all my clients and as the original deal slowly got chipped away, I left (I remember telling the boss, "I work to live, not live to work"; one of the rare times when I came up with a good line when I needed it.)

Before leaving HK, a buddy I had met there planted the idea of going to China to learn Chinese. I believe the conversation was, "Hey, if you have nothing better to do, go to China, learn Chinese. The university there is a blast and China's the future, man".

Well, I didn't have anything better to do, I did go, the university was a blast and China is the future.

Oh, before making it to China I did manage to squeeze in one year living in Kwangju, Korea, and a whole different world opened up for me. In Hong Kong, everything is high-stress, steel and concrete, and money, money, money! You always feel like you're not going fast enough to keep up, that you're missing something by being here now, doing this now. Everyone scurries. Everyone lives life in fast-forward.

By contrast, Kwangju is a city of a million people with a small-town, thoroughly Korean atmosphere. I had a blast. Not because teaching English was so much fun, but because of the great people I met and because I took Tae Kwon Do in the morning, trained with the Korean

Archery team in the afternoon and took Hapkido in the evening. It was a very cool year.

That year was plenty of time to figure out that work isn't all it's cracked up to be, so I decided to go back to school to become a professor of comparative mythologies. I found the books by Joseph Campbell absolutely fascinating.

This was my plan: be in China for four years; learn Chinese for two years, with another two years on a Master's degree in Oriental Philosophy, then go to graduate school in the U.S.

I flew from Korea to Beijing, arriving in China on a gray, rainy September day in 1995.

Section II

Boot Camp

When you can walk across this rice paper Grasshopper…

8. THIS TIME, YOU'RE THE 'F.O.B.'

F.O.B — Fresh off the Boat (not Freight on Board)

In North America there is a somewhat condescending saying people use for immigrants or overseas students who have just arrived to America and have no idea about ... anything. They walk around a little lost, all the time.

How appropriate that saying is for the hoards of business types that come over to China. Yet, where the fresh students know they don't have a clue, the business types don't yet know they don't have a clue.

Let's just get past that part as quickly as we can.

You need to be prepared and you need to overcome the three "I's":

Inexperience, impatience and immaturity:

1. **Inexperience** with doing business in China

2. **Impatience** with dealing with all that you will have to deal with here and

3. **Immaturity** with thinking you know enough already or that you won't make the same mistakes other people have made.

So grasshopper, if you can't walk across this rice paper without leaving tracks, you cannot/*should not* leave the monastery.

You are reading this book, great.

And you really should keep reading others; if nothing, but to get other perspectives. There is no one China Business Bible.

I certainly don't have ALL the answers.

I have some insights and have made lots of mistakes which I will share with you so you don't have to make the same mistakes I made (you can go make all new ones).

And just as you would expect, training for something greatly improves your odds of success compared to jumping right in and hoping you will be a virtuoso.

There is no guarantee you'll win... but you are improving your odds (Like getting dealt at least one ace in every hand of Texas Hold'em).

9. BORN TO BE SCHIZO

Communist Dogma & a Cultural basis in wealth...A façade of superiority with an inferiority complex...

The Chinese have been brought up to be schizophrenic. They were told over and over again as children that the Chinese are the best around, but they have grown up seeing that Western countries have more and are more technologically advanced than them. That's a lot for a kid's brain to handle.

And that's just the start.

Just about everyone older than 35 grew up in or surrounded by unbelievable poverty and with a "Let's work together as a people for the people" refrain banging into their brains, courtesy of the Communist Party; while at the same time being driven by an internal drive for riches. (The #1 Holiday, Chinese New Year, everyone greets each other with "Hope you get rich next year")

So as soon as they were given the opportunity (Deng Xiao Ping's, "rich is good" comment), they jumped out of the starter gates like a bat outta hell. Basically everything they grew up hearing in school and told to them by people in positions of authority doesn't jive with the times.

Those who are still in power dance this bizarre dance where the words coming out of their mouth and the song playing in the background don't really match what their feet are doing. But they are in power, so those politically astute business people pretend this is natural and applaud as they go.

How could you not be schizophrenic, living and doing business in such an environment? You would be. I would be. As someone not used to this environment, you'd better understand this situation or you will never survive.

It's crazy, man.

It's like a whole different planet.

10. DOING BUSINESS ON PLANET MEYNLAND

Imagine you have landed on another planet, ready to do business.

Let's call it Planet Meynland.

This planet has a livable environment inhabited by human beings just like you. In fact, it's a lot like your home planet. But there are so many people all vying for the same resources that the competition is necessarily fiercer. In the jungle mentality, survival is top priority. Social niceties would be nice but are NOT a priority.

To make matters worse (or more confusing, anyway!), the people on this planet have been taught an entirely different way of thinking. Since they've been taught differently, they think differently. And because they think differently, they act differently. So, just when you think you're getting the hang of them, they do something so totally unexpected and you realize you don't have the first clue.

Be aware of two critical realities.   One, the Meynland business environment is hostile.   It's "survival of the fittest" in action.   Second, the business environment is confusing - even more confusing than it seems at first glance. *It looks and sounds a lot like Western business environments, but it runs according to somewhat different principles.*

Worth repeating: In the West people are taught the ends do NOT justify the means. On this planet, many business people may give that lip service, but practice the opposite and the ends DO IN FACT justify the means (so long as one doesn't get caught and lose face.)

Be advised: most consider lying, cheating and stealing as black and white concepts. Not so much here. They fall into more of a gray zone and are only "bad" if people 1. Find out and 2. See them as bad. The appearance of being "good" is good enough.

Back on Earth...overall the Chinese people are warm, wonderful and fascinating. And they are cold, nasty and rude. In short, they are folks like all the rest of us. People are people everywhere, of course.

So when you are doing business in Mainland China, you might want to remind yourself from time to time that you are doing it on an entirely different planet – because, in many ways, you are.

11. CHINA'S OTHER GREAT WALL

The plane touches down, and the wonder and excitement are palpable. Another load of China virgins has arrived.

Some are newly-minted college graduates or MBAs. Some are experienced guerilla entrepreneurs who made their bones in successful enterprises in the West. Some are fast-rising corporate hotshots who've been sent to expand their organization's interests into this exotic, ancient land, or rescue a drowning subsidiary from... well, *drowning*.

But all are looking for love – in the form of money, money, money. All are strangers in an even stranger land. A fascinating, *seductive* land. And in no time, they are seduced.

You'll be no different, my friend.

The Forbidden City, the Great Wall, the Summer Palace, Peking duck banquets, and acrobats will inspire and enthrall you. The dancers, musicians, artists, museums, shopping, the gorgeous karaoke girls - and the sheer number of people! – will have your head spinning in no time. The friendly faces and warm smiles will make you feel as though you're among friends.

And before you know it, you will fall in love.

Thanks to your infatuated state, your first few weeks of life in China will be overwhelming and exhausting... and unbelievably thrilling. And just as it did when you fell in love in high school, the thrill will fade with time.

If you can experience this romance with the wise eyes of one who's aware of love's fantasies and follies, there's a good chance you'll be able to hold on to your sanity (and possibly even a profit margin) doing business in China.

Even after you hit the Great Wall.

Oh, the wall! The wall! The wall! The wall you are going to hit going 100 miles an hour at some point. I feel for you! The wall I'm talking about is not the famed Great Wall* of China, but the psychological wall you're going to run into after you've been in China somewhere between months four and eight.

Everything in this book is designed to help you pick yourself up off the ground afterward, bloodied but unbroken... but nothing I can do will save you from the collision itself.

What happens is this...

---

* As for the real, genuine, certified Great Wall... yes, it is really, really, really long – and no, you can't see it from space with the naked eye. Sorry.

The unadulterated romance period that I talked about, lasts about two or three months. After that, you start noticing that your new love (China) has a few nasty habits. People spit in public. They pick their noses in restaurants. They refuse to stand in lines. They push and shove. They stare.

The Water Torture is working on you. Everything gets under your skin. It makes you nuttier and nuttier, until somewhere between four and eight months in, you hit THE WALL. You have had enough. You become irritable and short with people, not a nice person to be around. Things come out of your mouth that you will wish you could lick back up. You break the Golden Rule one too many times and decide you do not want to be this person, this monster China has made you, any longer.

That's when you know it's time to get out.

Fine. Get out.

But don't give up! Don't make a decision to pull up stakes and leave based on this experience – The Great Wall. Just take a break, my friend.

Then, get back on that plane and head back to the frustrating place you'll have discovered has got its hooks in you, like a woman who's no good for you but you can't forget. And do some more business!

After that, take a break every 2-3 months.

No, just do it. Make it a priority. Consider it a cost of doing business.

** For those experienced expatriates, the other Great Wall is my version of culture shock.

12. CHINA'S 5000 YEAR HISTORY IN UNDER 200 WORDS.

It's LONG, over 5000 years.

Something they are very proud of and rightly so.

The Chinese invented papermaking, printing, gunpowder, and the compass (and depending who you ask, pretty much everything else worthwhile).

China had the best navy in the world in the 15th Century. Sailed the world long before everyone else, saw they were more advanced and decided, "Forget the barbarians."

They dismantled their navy and stayed indoors for the next few centuries while everyone then surpassed them.

Then the foreigners came, forced themselves in really; bringing opium.

An agreement was reneged on and lots of stuff was burned, leaving the Chinese with an embarrassing "scar" which is still remembered and which now translates into the deep-seated belief that "you foreigners owe us."

13. THEY'RE relatively NEW TO THIS

Imagine a country where the market economy has been around for centuries. Buying, selling, manufacturing, and distribution systems have been created and honed in a competitive atmosphere. Because of this, the best product or service is much more likely to win over the competition. So, companies have learned to be vigilant, always striving to improve and innovate - or risk annihilation.

As a result, business leaders have gathered a vast store of knowledge which they have passed on (and continue to pass on) to the next generation through books, business schools, mentoring, and research grants. So, more than a few young people in this economy leave college with the condensed wisdom of the leadership of the most successful businesses and insights of great research crammed into their heads.

Now, picture a second country where all business acumen was wiped clean for more than 30 years. Business leaders were killed or driven into hiding. Libraries were burned. Universities were gutted. And intellectuals, researchers and teachers were humiliated, executed and replaced with uneducated workers and political fanatics – if they were replaced at all.

For 30 years, there was no competition, no innovation, no forward movement, no reason to improve and no incentive to do a better job or sell more widgets. In fact, anything to do with business was dirty, evil and illegal.

So, when the country re-opened to commerce, business education and experience was nowhere to be found. Most people didn't have a clue about what to do next.

The first country is the West. The second is of course, China.

Now, don't get me wrong. Many Chinese are at their core uber-entrepreneurs; I'm not talking about the ones you know, those who have either been living in the West or maybe Hong Kong, Taiwan or Singapore.

I'm talking about the Mainland Chinese.

You saw the 2008 Summer Olympics; the Chinese are learning fast. And in 25 years from now, the new generation may be in a position similar to their peers in the West. But right now, the China business world is flooded with inexperienced people of all ages who are basically winging it every day. After all, the Chinese market only opened up a couple dozen years ago, with Deng Xiao Ping's, "Rich is OK" policy.

I say this because it is important for you to realize that the people with whom you are going to make deals will not share the same assumptions and business "givens" as you.

They're learning as they go, in a marketplace that is basically on steroids, growing so fast that even the West's most educated and experienced corporate officers would have a tough time keeping up with it.

This reality will dramatically impact all of your experiences while doing business in China, but there are three major areas of your business it will impact every day:

- You'll have a tough, tough time finding experienced managers. And, you might not be able to afford to hire or keep those you find anyway, since large, monied corporations tend to snap them up and pay them very well.

- Your most ambitious, talented employees won't necessarily take the "long view" when it comes to slogging out the tough times out with you while you're small, so you can all enjoy the wealth when you're big. They're still in "get it while the getting's good" survival mode, left over from their earlier days – and opportunity seems to be popping up all over.

- You will have to train, train, train most of your new hires in business; elementary customer-service skills such as treating customers like gold, being courteous and respectful to their fellow workers, keeping things neat and clean, and carrying out their assigned responsibilities faithfully. And many, many more.

THIS IS BLANK ON PURPOSE

One day you will understand.

15. DON'T BLAME MAO, CONFUCIUS SCREWED THEM FIRST

What do you get when you convince millions of people that the path to happiness is submission to authority, keeping one's place and overall social conformity? You get a nation full of people who tow the line and swallow anger, injustice and their dreams.

Confucianism was China's Standard Operating Procedure, the way everyone agreed that society should work, for more than 2000 years. Communism came and went in a matter of decades, but Confucianism held its ground the whole time. It reigned supreme in the hearts and habits of the Chinese people, if not in their minds or their mouths. It melded with the Communist political system and even strengthened it.

It's a seemingly mild-mannered philosophy started by a scholar who was no doubt well-intentioned, but whose ideas laid the groundwork for massive exploitation and suppression of those with less status by those with *more*.

Confucius taught that all relationships (except, supposedly, those between friends) are naturally hierarchical, with one person being the leader and the other being subordinate. Though Confucius admonished that all *people* are equal, when his theories are put into practice, they create a completely inequitable social system. One person is automatically considered superior and the other inferior in any given interaction or relationship. Even friends who are supposed to have equal status in regard to each other, never really do. A complicated calculation of who is older, better educated, from a better family, etc., will determine who is on top in the relationship and who is not.

In Confucianism, husbands "outrank" wives, older children outrank younger children, and boys always outrank girls. Rulers are rulers by divine right and ought not be questioned or challenged – and the same goes for employers, the government and anyone with power.

And business? Commerce? That was the dirt and muck of society.

According to Confucius, scholars deserve society's highest ranking, followed by farm workers who gain their dignity from providing food for the people as a whole. Subordinate to farm workers are artists, whose work is considered somewhat frivolous (and more enjoyable). At the very bottom of the heap are merchants, or business people. Yes, Confucius considered business people the dregs of humanity – at least in regard to their work.

And up until very recently, profit only occurred through "exploiting" the workers.

China is full of talented, brilliant people who must constantly juggle their own ideas and rights to others because of deeply-ingrained Confucian culture. And the Chinese business world is full of people who have been taught one thing in school, but are then required to act completely differently at work.

Confucius screwed them over, man.

16. IT'S ALL ABOUT FACE

Getting past the great people you will meet and work with here, if I had to describe the secret to the biggest chunk of the Chinese market in as few words as possible, it would be the following equation:

$$\frac{\text{Appearance}}{\text{Substance}}$$

Appearance over substance.

Yes, that is a sweeping statement.

Yes, there are plenty of people who will be shocked and want to argue it.

Don't bother. Move on.

This is a comment about the behavior of the market not about individuals.

I know a lot of Westerners that interpret the concept of "face", to mean "respect." I wish face was synonymous with respect, but it's not. In most situations, face is just like it sounds: shallow. "Face" primarily is about surface issues and interactions; ergo, appearance over substance. Do not think that surface issues and interactions aren't important, because here they ABSOLUTELY are.

Bottom-line, 'face' cares more about appearances than actual substance.

If you understand *face*, you can comprehend and navigate thousands of social and business situations that simply make no sense without it.

Remember:
It's not just what you do, but *how* you do it.

Did you buy an expensive enough dinner? (If they actually liked it, doesn't really matter.) Where you eat and the dishes you order are possibly more important than the food itself.

Remember:
It's not just what you say, but *how* you say it.

Did you *say* the right things? (What you *thought* doesn't really matter.)

In fact, you can give someone you despise lots and lots of face, and both of you will still know exactly what you really think about them. You'll play your role and they'll play theirs. And it will all mean nothing, except that the status quo is being maintained.

But wait, there's more...

There are 2 sides to this "Face" coin. "Giving face" to others, you can pretty much control and is much easier than NOT making others "lose face."

Let me put it on the table: losing face is a Chinese person's BIGGEST fear.

In other words, NOT losing face is the number one motivator for just about everyone and everything in China; followed closely by the number two motivator, finding ways to gain face.

This is a major theme and by the end of this book, you will see how often this will affect your business.

So what does this mean to you?

1. When it comes to "giving face," if you don't have someone to arrange it for you, at least check with an experienced local, preferably some "business development" person, before choosing where to go for dinner and what to order. This goes double if any "gifts" are involved. Plenty has been written about the cultural blunders you can make, like giving clocks or using the #4...look it up.

2. Avoid things that make people "lose face." Most common mistakes: being critical, pointing out mistakes, taking the superior tone. Being humble goes a long way

here. When in doubt, be diplomatic, rather than straightforward.

That being said...

Arrogance is often seen by people here as being strong and strength is respected.

Read on and it will become clearer.

17. EVERYTHING THAT'S NOT ABOUT FACE, IS ABOUT GUANXI

Guanxi (pronounced: *gwan shee*) sounds like something magical. Something mystical. Perhaps an ancient Chinese value, custom or tradition. It sounds exotic, esoteric, even spiritual. It's not.

It is connections, pure and simple. Name-dropping squared.

You've heard the phrase, "It's not what you know, it's who you know." Well, this is about ten times as true in China as it is anywhere else in the world. Here, who you know has a lot to do with how successful you'll be in any given endeavor. You can be sure someone with a lot of Guanxi has friends in key, influential or high places, and knows how to use them.

Why is Guanxi so important? Well, my personal theory that it's because trust is so rare and hard to earn around here. So, each and every connection you have naturally becomes that much more important in and of itself – as well as an implication that you can be trusted.

You often need Guanxi to help you jump through the thousands of bureaucratic hoops the government has laid out for you.

You definitely need Guanxi to meet the potential partners and prospects who could make you successful, wealthy or powerful.

You usually need Guanxi to survive, to stay in business and to see your company's objectives met and exceeded.

Guanxi works the same in China as everywhere else. Some people are born into it. Some people are introduced to or become friends with it. Some people buy it. Nothing mystical there. Name dropping in business is not pretentious in China, it's just good for business.

On the other side, whenever someone gets nailed for wrongdoing in politics, the typical Chinese thinking is, it's not because they did something wrong (they are always doing something wrong). It's because they did something that could be interpreted as "wrong" and did not have enough Guanxi to protect themselves – or they were outplayed by an enemy or competitor with better Guanxi.

18. YOU CAN ALWAYS GET MORE GUANXI

If you are not born into Guanxi or marry into it, you can be introduced to it by business acquaintances, friends, hired guns, or a new romantic partner. You can hire full-time team members or retain consultants with lots of connections.

You can even buy it, straight out – and that's a darn good thing, because you need Guanxi to get even the simplest things done. All you have to do is find somebody who knows somebody and compensate them for hooking you up (or backing you up, as the case may be). You'll call them a "consultant," but the only consulting they may do is calling their cousin whose girlfriend's father knows the licensing commissioner.

The good news is you can also cultivate your own Guanxi. And you will if you're smart and do nice things for the people you do business with, for or around.

You know that small-time official who's giving you trouble about violating Section 1425 of Code C-6? Does his son need to practice his English? Invite him to work with the English tutor you've hired for your staff at no charge. Does his daughter need help getting into college overseas? Introduce him to someone who can pull some strings for her.

Now, let me be very clear: Bribes of any kind are out. They are against the law, and you don't want to end up in a Chinese prison, believe me. But "gifts" are fine.

Don't demand quid pro quo; simply perform an act of "kindness" or put to work on their behalf whatever Guanxi you already have, with no (visible) strings attached. Then, watch the magic happen.

19. CHINESE WATER TORTURE

According to ancient lore, in Chinese water torture, the victim is immobilized, lying prone, while water slowly drips onto his forehead for hours or even days, inevitably driving him insane.

While my extensive research (two minutes - Wikipedia) shows there's no evidence that Chinese water torture has ever actually been used by the Chinese, I can tell you this: it's the perfect metaphor for what often happens to you in China.

Life in China is exciting and often wonderful. It's also the definition of "stressful", when you're trying to launch a product or accomplish anything of value in the business world.

Don't be afraid, it's not stressful in a "How can these people be so mean?" kind of a way. Most people are quite courteous even kind.

Nor is it stressful in a "We can't possibly overcome this hurdle" kind of a way. Because 99% of the time, you'll know you can – with some strategy, hard work or a little bit of Guanxi.

Doing business in China is stressful in an "Are you f^%king kidding me? If one more of these little nagging mosquito of a problem comes up, I am going to take a dull spoon and cut my heart out, because it has been months and months of nothing but tiny little problems, and I just can't take it anymore!" kind of a way.

It's Chinese water torture.

So now that you know this, be prepared.

See Chapter 88, "Hire a Handler."
See Chapter 49, "Staying Power."

20. CHINESE FIRE DRILLS

When I was a kid, we used to do Chinese fire drills in the car. We'd get to a red light and someone would yell "Chinese fire drill!" We'd all jump out, run around the car, and pile back into the same spots we'd occupied before. The object of the game was to be exactly where we started before the light turned green.

Lots of movement. Lots of activity. No progress. Zero.

As a kid, this was tremendous fun. In hindsight, though, it was kind of a derogatory title for a game that focused on useless activity. (Not to mention that it isn't something I'd advise. Keep your seatbelts on, kids!) At the same time, the way the game played out really rings true when it comes to a certain kind of experience you are going to have while you're in China. I mean that. It's not a question of "if." It's a question of "when."

Here's what happens. You've been brought in to trouble-shoot for your corporation in China. Your company's counting on you to fix something that's broken. Or you've looked at your own business and seen the light about some things you need or want to change.

So, you get together with your team and come up with some exciting new goals, new ways of doing things, new visions.

Rah-rah-rah! Everyone's pumped. Everyone's excited. You included!

You go home and tell your wife or husband what a great meeting you just had. Then, for weeks or months, you watch everyone run around, seemingly busy making things happen. Eventually, you look up and realize that nothing much has happened. You are pretty much where you were when you started. Or even exactly where you were when you started.
Poop.

What happened?

Chinese Fire Drill.

Maybe you were sabotaged from the inside. Maybe your communication wasn't clear enough. Maybe you didn't realize people rarely ask questions here. Maybe, maybe, maybe…

You can bet that in nine cases out of ten, your team really wanted to pull it out for you. They just couldn't, and here's why:

They needed to ask questions but didn't. They're living in a high-context culture which teaches them that they should just know what you're trying to communicate to them – even though you're from a different culture altogether and totally suck at communicating with them.

They kept their mouths shut to save your face – and theirs. You've heard the (stupid and totally wrong) saying "Love means never having to say you're sorry." Well, face means doing everything "right" and having all the answers. So, when your team members were confused and didn't know what to do next, they tried to protect you from looking like an incompetent manager - and themselves from looking like incompetent employees.

They really, honestly, thought they were doing what you wanted them to do. That's how badly you suck at communicating with Chinese people, my friend.

You can avoid (most!) Chinese fire drills by setting small, measurable goals on your way to the larger goal. Create baby steps that will get your team members where they need to go – and baby-sit your employees on the way. Not because they're incompetent or irresponsible, but because you are not Chinese and don't have the first clue about communicating effectively with them.

21. THE CHINA PRICE

You can't beat the Chinese on price. Don't even try. If you go up against them, they will grind your face in the dirt and leave you broke, shivering and convinced you're a loser before you know what's happening.

Even when you start producing your products here, they will still probably be able to effectively produce the same products at 30% cheaper than you.

Why?

Is it because you are a foreigner?

Is it because there is some conspiracy against you?

Yes and No.

Here's the sad, all-too-common scenario. A foreign entrepreneur comes to China to set up shop. He looks around and finds a manufacturer for his product and gets a price quote. He is amazed and pleased to hear a number that is at least 30% cheaper than he'd pay at home. After a bit of bargaining, the price is 35% cheaper, and he's stoked. He finds a great location to sell his wares and bargains with the landlord until his rent is 40% less than it would be for a comparable storefront in the U.S. Life is good. The whole time the entrepreneur is thinking what a great deal they're getting... all the while comparing it to prices *back home*. (MISTAKE #1)

The same routine, but done by a local entrepreneur, WILL get up to 30% cheaper because their perspective is DIFFERENT. They will bargain harder, cut out stuff that a foreigner HAS TO HAVE and pretty much squeeze every cent they can out of everything.

Boom!
They are already starting out with cheaper costs.

And THAT is the main reason why you will never beat the Chinese on price.

Cutting corners, cheaper materials, lower labour costs, and copying versus innovating are the typical complaints, but when you get beat at your own game, this difference in cost perspective is the one that usually gets overlooked.

There's a popular idea in a lot of self-help and motivational circles that anything you can believe, you can achieve. Well, you can "believe" all you want, but you cannot out-bargain a native Chinese competitor. You simply can't. You cannot beat the Chinese on price.

So repeat after me: "I can't beat the Chinese on price."
　　"I can't beat the Chinese on price."
　　"I can't beat the Chinese on price."
　　"I can't beat the Chinese on price."

Now I bet there are a number of you out there who will take this chapter as a challenge instead of a lesson. I'm sorry (for you) to hear that. BUT, I am willing to completely refund the cost of this book if you manage to actually beat the Chinese on price.

What I mean by this is if twelve months AFTER you start beating them on price, you are *still* beating them on price, let me know. I figure you have four to six months before a competitor pops up and BEATS YOU ON PRICE!

22. REMEMBER, YOU ARE IN THEIR SANDBOX

AKA Mind Your Manners

From the moment your airplane lands, think of yourself as a guest in China's house and live that way until you get back on the plane to head home.

That includes watching your mouth like it's a loaded gun when it comes to your political opinions. If you can't say something nice about China or the Chinese government, just smile and nod your head. In general, it's best to keep all of your political opinions to yourself, like they're your ATM pin code or your ex-girlfriend's photos.

To the West, Democracy is a beautiful thing. Democracy is all about speaking your truth freely and fully. Democracy is what we are used to living, breathing and expounding on in clubs, cocktail parties, weddings and bar mitzvahs.

China is not a democracy.

And before you get all uptight, remember you are visiting **their** house and *no one* likes to be told how they should live their life. Throwing stones....glass houses.... Ahem....

Oh yeah, Chinese folks can be very, very touchy about the "Ts."

> Don't talk about Taiwan.
> Don't talk about Tibet.
> Don't talk about Tiananmen Square.

Even a close friend or lover is likely to get extremely ticked off at you if you make value judgments about any of the above. Bringing them up at all is an etiquette no-no on your part.

If I were stupid enough to *want* to fight with my wife, choosing from the above menu of options would be the fast track.

If you're inclined to be frustrated by this state of affairs, remember that the Chinese have substantial emotional and social investments in toeing the party line. In China, activism is not an option the way it is in other parts of the world. So, philosophical discussions about politics and political actions are guaranteed to be just that: philosophical.

In the end, respect for your friends and colleagues should be your guide. Why would you want to risk embarrassing or angering the people around you when there's just no point?

Just remember that you are not in China to agitate for reform, but to make money (honestly and ethically, of course), and you'll do fine.

23. KICK ASS OR KISS ASS

As we already stated, everything in China is about face and the main factor in determining who is the giver and who is the receiver is POWER: either who has it and who doesn't or, who has more. This mental calculation is done at the beginning of every relationship, every social interaction, everything.

If you are not in the dominant position and you want something, you'd better pucker up. If you don't, you can either expect nothing to get accomplished or a can of whoop ass to be opened just for you.

There's no such thing as social equality as we understand and prize it in the West, communist party rhetoric aside. Whenever two or more Chinese are gathered together, one has the upper hand. And just about everyone accepts this state of affairs as normal and natural.

Want examples? Read *Journey to the West*, a book detailing and celebrating the exploitative adventures of the Monkey King, or watch just about any Chinese pop-culture movie. The use, mis-use and abuse of power aren't just portrayed time and time again. They're romanticized, even celebrated.

So, what does this mean for you? It means that power plays, sabotage and exploitative business practices are tolerated and even endorsed by many Chinese as "part of the game." Think office politics taken a few steps closer to mafia politics. It's not personal. It's business. So watch your back if you're corporate and be aware of how your staff are behaving.

Be advised that clashes between employees happen when it is unclear who has the upper hand and THAT is the second most popular reason your staff need very clear job descriptions. (First reason is so they know what is *not* their responsibility and therefore know how to avoid losing face.)

24. DO...YOU...UNDERSTAND...ME!!!????

"Your lips move, but I can't hear what you're sayin."
-Pink Floyd, Comfortably Numb

Quick Story:
I know an advertising executive who did several projects for a major Chinese organization. At the completion of each of the first two, he received a warm, simple thank you. After he finished the third, a slogan, the thanks were effusive, to say the least. "Oh, we love it! It's wonderful! You work so hard for us! We are very happy! It's very creative!"

Glowing praise was heaped upon glowing praise. My pal, who has a fragile ego, was quite flattered, to say the least. Actually, he was thrilled with their response and what it might mean for their future business relationship.

At the end of the conversation, just as he thought they were about to wish each other a good afternoon, his contact said, "Mr. R---- asks if you would be so kind to look at something he wrote and see if there are any errors. I will fax it to you now, and you can send us a bill for fixing it."

"Certainly!" the executive replied. Since the organization had many fascinating interests, he was curious to see his assignment.

When it arrived, he couldn't believe his eyes! It was clearly a slogan intended to replace the one his contact had praised so highly. Why hadn't they told him they were unhappy with what he'd written? After all, he'd let the company know he'd be happy to create a new one if they weren't happy with the first – at no extra charge.

But he took his cues from his contact, cleaned up a spelling error and faxed it back with a note that he would be honored if they would accept his edit at no charge. They quite happily accepted his "kind generosity" and used their slogan instead of his.

After that, he was quite relieved and happy when he turned in projects and received a warm, simple thank you!

So what happened?

Most people will talk about "face" and how they were letting my buddy 'save face'. That is probably partially right. However there is an aspect of Chinese communication that you have to know

China, like most Asian nations, is what's called a "high-context" culture. In a "high-context" culture, the *least* important communication tool is words. What *really* matters is everything that happens around the words: the place where you are when they're spoken, the particulars of the situation, the person who's talking, and all their body language. It's even more about what someone *doesn't* say than what they *do say*.

Western cultures, like the U.S., are taught to value the importance of nonverbal signals. Well, multiply that importance when you're communicating with the Chinese 10 or 12 times, and you'll be on the right track.

The U.S., Canada and most Western nations are predominantly "low-context" cultures. The words we speak or write are meaningful in and of themselves, and the context in which they're said takes a much lower priority in our interpretations (although it still has importance, of course!).

Here's how communication works in China:

Person A has a thought they want to communicate to Person B.

Person A attempts to clearly express that thought.

Person B filters Person A's message using the lifetime learned skills of "What they really mean is"...

So be prepared after you give someone clear, concise, laser beam focused instructions and they immediately reply back, "OK. So what you mean is...." And then proceed to re-interpret what you thought to be simple and clear into something totally different.

On a bad day, this is going to make you want to scream.

But be advised this is really a **good** thing, because it's better than NOT telling you what "you think," doing something different and then leaving you to find out later. (This too will happen a lot.)

Think positive.

25. GETTING AROUND THE POINT

Westerners like to get right to the point, operating in an efficient "straight line" way. Chinese... not so much. Remember, the ends justify the means here, meaning the process is not always viewed as important, as long as you get what you want.

So be prepared because there WILL absolutely be times when you feel like things are going off on a tangent or that people are taking unnecessary steps to get something done. It may be because they are inefficient, (that certainly happens a lot around here and with over 1.3 billion people around, inefficiency means more people have jobs) or it's simply things happening the way they 'need' to here.

Rarely can you follow a straight line path to get to where you want to be.

Sammies moment
When Sammies wanted to open cafés downtown, I was told we would not be able to get the licenses because small time WOFE's (Wholly Owned Foreign Enterprises) couldn't open multiple retail food locations.

The brilliant woman (local Chinese) who had set up my venture for $2,000 USD said we could, however set up locations under our manufacturing license since we were selling our own products. Bottom line, we did have to jump through an obstacle course, but it got done.

(Wait for Chapter 28)

26. THE 2 MOST UNCOMMON THINGS IN CHINA

1. Common Sense

It seems to me that foreigners, when they do business in China, seem to think that what would normally be common sense back home, just doesn't apply here.

If your due diligence finds something strange or your would-be partner gives you a bad vibe, LISTEN! Don't think just because you are on the opposite side of the globe that business in China should operate on some sort of Bizarro-world rules.

From another perspective, don't think your staff is stupid because they don't think like you. They did not grow up in the same system surrounded by the same things as you and they were taught different things. So they will approach problems differently.

2. Common Courtesy

I am not talking about the uncommon courtesy you will find in the 5-star hotels or the upscale restaurants. That may blow your mind and have you thinking how far behind the West is in this regard.

I am talking about what you will find, or not find for that matter, while walking on the street. You will rarely find that people hold doors open or say they are sorry when walking through a crowded street and they knock into you. I do not know if this is a result of so many people (back to the "Jungle" mentality) or a face issue, but you will inevitably bump into these situations.

Your ability to brush it off and choose not to let it get under your skin will serve you very well.

27. ALL FOREIGNERS LOOK THE SAME

To the eyes of the untrained Westerner, most Asians look too similar to differentiate; which, not too surprisingly, can be insulting to Orientals. To be fair and for some fun, check out www.alllooksame.com and take the face test. Everyone I know has done about the same, Chinese and other.

As in most places, there is a standard disposition between Chinese and non-Chinese. Don't think that the Chinese have a simple "us and them" attitude because there is also a deep-seated mental calculation for other ethnically Chinese, based on where you are from.

First there is by country; Chinese from Singapore, Hong Kong, or Taiwan tend to look down on the Mainlanders and oddly enough, the Mainlanders don't really like being looked down on, leaving a bit of tension always hanging there. The tension is certainly not as bad as with other races, but be advised: do not expect your ethnically Chinese "transplant" to be welcomed with open arms when they arrive in China.

But wait there's more...

There also exists the calculation based on where someone is from *within* China. What province and even what city? Ask any Chinese about the different provincial stereotypes and you will get the usual: Shandong people are nice, Henan people are sly etc. The real kicker is the different attitude between the urban and rural Chinese.

In the West there is certainly a perceived difference between the rural and urban dwellers. On the one hand you have the salt-of-the-Earth, like-a-rock, Ma and Pa Kettle-type farmers who may not appear as "slick" as the city dwelling, suit wearing corporate types, but the lifestyle they have is respected and even romanticized in the movies. On the other hand there's also the country-bumpkin stereotype, but overall, it's quite a balanced view.

In China, there is not such a balance.

If you want to insult a person, you call them a farmer (*nong min*). Actually, "farmer" is not the most appropriate translation, "peasant" is really the more exact meaning and bottom line: the city Chinese don't really like them.

They are seen as the unwashed, uncouth, and uneducated.

They are the nose pickers, the stare-at-you-with-their-mouth-open types, and the cross-the-highway-looking-the-wrong-way types. Peasants in China are all over the cities now as the construction crews, the street sweepers, the garbage picker-uppers, and they are viewed pretty much negatively, all around.

The rural Chinese are the low men on the totem pole and they too, do not like to be looked down upon. The way they get back at the arrogant city folk is to *not* look both ways as they slowly walk across the street, forcing the cars to slow down, to continue to stare at you and basically have a thick, thick skin for everything that goes on around them.

Oh yeah, the rural population represents about 70% and is one of the major factors that would make democracy next to impossible.

28. BEIJING SAMMIES – GETTING STARTED

I came back to Beijing with a scholarship to school and the burning desire to start a café. This year I knew enough about the system to make sure my roommate was a student who *didn't* live on campus, thereby giving me a single room.

I was 25 and wanted to get started. I needed a location and I needed a Chinese partner to help with the "official" stuff that I knew had to be taken care of. There were a few clubs and bars around the school that had been started by foreigners. Every one of them had a Chinese partner. (No, none of them are still around today)

My Chinese 'best friend' was from Qingdao so didn't have the right *"hu-kou"* (the residence permit required to live and work in an area.) to do business in Beijing. I had another Chinese friend who was keen to make some money and thought the idea was good. (I invest all the money, do all the work and he takes care of the government stuff for 25%.)

We looked around and had a number of fruitless meetings with the "head" of the marketplace. At this stage, I had only one year of studying under my belt, there was still a heck of a lot of vocabulary I didn't understand, so I was pretty much useless in all the meetings. I remember looking around at the dimly lit office with the dirty walls and thinking, "This can't be good." But, no, come on. This is China, be a little flexible. You can't expect it to be like back home.

I was told to be patient. We needed to become friends first. We needed to get some Guanxi with this guy. So somewhere between our third and sixth meeting, we bought him a bottle of expensive alcohol and left it in his office after one of our meetings.

When we returned the next week, the present was in the same spot. He didn't take it, so he owed us nothing. In hindsight there was no way we would get a spot. He may be the head of the marketplace, but he was still a low man on a larger totem pole and just couldn't take such an obvious risk, letting a white kid start a business in his backyard. Had I been Asian, we probably would have got a place. There already were a number of Korean/Chinese ventures in the area.

So after three months of no progress, my "partner" took a job that actually paid him money and I was back to square one.

It was shortly after this that my best buddy suggested that I partner with his cousin, who *was* from Beijing. He was a few years older and had a business before. We talked a bit. I didn't really like him, but he was my best friend's cousin, so… (yeah, yeah, you already know how this ends and it's not like I was the first or last person to make this mistake.)

We did put together a partnership agreement. (What a load of crap that was. Hmmm... let's see... You want to make a legally binding contract for an illegal company. Yeah. That makes sense.) The lawyer who put the contract together did tell me, when he was done, that he couldn't guarantee that the contract would be enforceable. So with that burst of confidence we got started!

After about a month we found a potential location. It was three units from one of the gates of the school; one of the gates that was currently closed, locked and never, EVER used. Honestly, before thinking about opening Sammies, I have no prior recollection that the gate was even there. But it **was** there and when the owner of the location said they would be opening it come summer, man-o-man was I excited.

The negotiation for that location was done over Erguotou, that nasty grain alcohol, which I can't stand to this day.

Not by me, but by my partner.

The two of them got absolutely shit-faced drunk in the process and a deal was struck. I watched the whole thing, not really comprehending what was being said half the time. The result was the owner of the location was going to rent the spot to us for slightly above what we wanted and we were to pay six months' rent. Not the best deal, but we wanted to get started.

Once we had signed the deal, it was time to um, actually start the businesses and I realized I that had no freaking clue what to do or where to start.

I had $25K to build everything. I talked with a few foreign construction companies that were way too expensive for my budget (I remember one guy telling me I didn't have enough money to call it a budget. He called it a midget-bidget) so we had to go local.

Lo and behold, my partner had a friend who did construction. We met. They took me out to dinner. We talked about the project and they would love to take it on. At this stage my partner took me aside and said he did not want to be a part of the negotiations on the price as they were his friends and that would have been uncomfortable for him.

(I cringe just thinking about this all now)

So I hired their crew and was super excited to get started. Then they asked me for the designs. Designs? Weren't you going to make the designs? I'll tell you what I want and you make the designs; right?

No. We're the construction company that builds. Show us the designs to build and we do that. That's all.

Enter Sam the Designer.

I bought some graph paper and made some drawings. Bought some more graph paper and made more drawings. Over the next week I spent zero hours on homework and all my time drawing, drawing, drawing.

I had to do everything. Floor layout. Tables, chairs. Counters, Kitchen design. I didn't know I was going to have to tell people where to put the plugs or how much electricity to put where. I almost lost it when they asked me where to put the lights (in the CEILING, you @$&% morons!)

But I must have done something right because the café was taking shape.

When we were half way done, the construction crew stopped work. They said it was tougher work than they anticipated and I needed to pay more. I looked to my friend. He looked out the window.

What was I going to do? Find another team to finish the job? Yeah, right... I was already paying rent and *had* to get it finished. I caved in, paid more and they got back to work.

By the time we finished and opened on May 13, 1997, we had barely enough money to pay 2 months' salary. We hadn't paid for the cash register and the air conditioner and the outdoor sign was only half paid for.

We should have gone out of businesses.

But we didn't. A number of the foreign students at the Beijing Language Institute (soon to become the Beijing Culture and Language University, BCLU) were also sick and tired of eating Chinese food 24/7.

Section III

Setting Yourself Up to Succeed

Being able to dress yourself and tie your own shoes.

29. YOUR TWO MOST IMPORTANT CHINA RULES

RULE #1
There's always a way.

RULE #2
There's always a better way.

These rules can, and should, be applied both positively and cynically.

Here's the positive way to apply these rules. First and foremost: be persistent. Sure you have hit a brick wall once, twice or a hundred times. But that doesn't mean whatever you are trying to do can't be done. It absolutely can be done. You just haven't figured out a way to do it yet.

So, don't give up. Get some help. Get a new plan. Then, (Rule #2) remember to stay flexible.

Once you think you've found a way to accomplish what you're trying to accomplish, don't lock yourself into that one course of action until you've looked around, spent a little more time thinking and asked yourself and others some tough questions. I'm not telling you to get stuck in "analysis paralysis." I am saying that really thinking it through will always pay off for you.

Here's the cynical way to apply these truths. Know that government officials may be paper pushers, but that doesn't mean they aren't creative. They can be accomplished artists at editing the truth, inventing regulations on the spot, making other rules and regulations disappear, and interpreting seemingly straightforward contracts in surprising ways.

But most of the time, they have to use their creativity to try to come up with some logical interpretation of what they should do with, to or for you, based on a shockingly illogical system of rules and regulations.

You can use both of these scenarios to your advantage, because it means nothing is ever really set in stone. It means that the bureaucrat who tells you, emphatically, that you are SOL and will be out of business in weeks may be only *half* full of crap. It means someone, somewhere, can probably be reasoned with, cajoled, flattered or finessed into making things go your way. It means that another bureaucrat may have another answer, another interpretation.

When things look bleak, don't get a lawyer. Get Guanxi. Find someone you know "who knows someone who knows someone" or hire a consultant with Guanxi to see how cheaply, easily and quickly things can be turned around by pulling the right strings.

There's always someone you can find to help you, or something you can offer to help him "reconsider." (Not a direct bribe!) And most of all, there's lots and lots and lots of face you can give him, which will soften his heart toward you.

In China, whenever someone gets nailed for wrongdoing in business, it's never because they did something wrong. It's because they did something that could be interpreted as "wrong" and did not have enough Guanxi to protect themselves.

They might even be the victim of a political plot dreamed up and carried out by an enemy or competitor with more Guanxi.

(By the way, I doubt there is any more corruption in China than there is anywhere else. It's just more "accessible" here to ordinary folks like you and me.)

30. DO YOUR FRICKIN' HOMEWORK

Before you go, read, read, read! Read everything you can find in reliable sources about entrepreneurship, markets and the state of your industry in China from the comfort of your cozy Western home.

Then, get off your duff and go see what's happening for yourself. Yes, visit China before you decide to live and work there. (This should go without saying, but an amazing number of people decide to start a business in China without spending time here first.)

Set aside a couple of weeks to spend time on the ground doing footwork, "hands-on" marketing research and simple "Could-I-really-handle-living-here" mental calculations. Find all the foreigners you can in your industry and ask them to mentor you. Collect horror stories. Ask people who got screwed exactly *why* and *how* they got screwed. Ask people who have survived, thrived and are thrilled to be living and working in China to tell you their stories.

Get advice from anyone who will let you buy them lunch. And really listen to everyone: the bitter, busted ones and the super-sonic successes. You'll be glad you did. (As for official China stats, put as much trust in them as you would directions from a drunk. They may be right, but verify them before you make decisions based on them.)

It's a jungle here, one where the ability to initiate contacts and ask for help or advice is a critical survival skill. If you're not an extrovert, you'd better partner with one, because alone, your chances are slim. Bounce your ideas off of people who've "been there, done that," and you'll avoid hundreds of mistakes that would be otherwise unavoidable.

And, just as important as all of the above information, get at least an elementary education in Chinese business philosophy. Start by reading *The Secret Art of War: the 36 Stratagems*. Follow that up with Lucien Pye's classic, *Chinese Negotiating Style*. (Some people think the art of negotiation was *invented* by the Chinese.)

By the way: if you jump in head first and discover there's no water in the pool, don't expect any sympathy from the Chinese. It will be, "too bad, so sad," because they do their homework. So maybe you'll get off your butt and take care of business before the red jungle takes care of *you*.

31. FORGET REMOTE CONTROL

Yes, you can set up your company, live in North America or Europe, and manage your business spending a week or so every month on site and handling the rest through conference calls and email.

Just don't expect your business to take off.

I have yet to meet anyone who has succeeded using a long-distance management style. Yes, it's becoming more and more popular and effective in the West, but it doesn't work in mainland China.

Doing business by remote control isn't a viable option for several reasons.

First, relationships are an integral part of how business gets done here. Folks here like to make deals eyeball to eyeball with people they know who also know other people they know. That's why cold-calling has never worked in China. And it's why even some of the West's biggest corporate names have left this place with their tail between their legs. They were spanked by an underdog competitor whose CEO took the time to really get to know the prospect and gave him lots of face by giving him lots of face time.

But that's not all. Because of the cultural acceptance of the attitude that "All's fair in war and business," subterfuge and sabotage – while they might be lowdown and dirty in a personal relationship – are considered a natural, even entertaining part of the business game. So, you just can't afford to leave your fate in the hands of others.

If your partners, employees and/or vendors are like the majority of Chinese who buy into this mindset (and at least some of them will be!), you can't afford not to keep your eyes, or the eyes of a highly-trusted, longtime ally, peeled for signs of trouble on a daily basis.

Remember: the fact that someone is on your payroll doesn't guarantee their loyalty. A true team member is someone you have good reason to trust is on your side, someone who has suited up, shown up, and played hard for you – even in the toughest of games.

Either you, someone with a significant vested interest in your success, or someone you'd trust with your wife, your kids, and your life need to be on the ground and overseeing your interests on a daily basis.

Your best bet for an on-the-ground person is someone whose success and personal satisfaction are tied up in your success and satisfaction – someone with a proven track record of valuing you and your interests over the temptations of short-term gain.

Sure, contract manufacturing and OEM agreements can help you keep things humming along with less involvement and oversight from you once you have strong relationships in place. You can judiciously make the most of them once you are large enough (and stable enough!) to weather the storms that will arise simply because you take a step back.

But while you're getting started and trying to build a solid foundation, you need to be crystal clear and completely in the know about everything that's going on in your China venture. You need someone with a vested interest in your survival to be on the ground.

You have been warned.

32.   BIGFOOT, YETIS & THE CHINA EXPERT

Have you ever heard of someone called an "America Expert"?

Of course not. That is too broad a title and if someone said that, you would think them arrogant beyond belief. Well, beware of the self proclaimed "China Expert." If you think I'm a China expert, it's only because you don't know enough about China and it's easy to impress you at this stage.

I'm talking about consultants.

From a positive perspective, you seek out consultants like you do doctors. Doctors have studied and after years of experience have seen and dealt with a number of different ills over and over again and are able to diagnose them quickly and hopefully "fix" them before they kill you. Consultants worth their salt have been in China for at least five years. They will not be theorizers, but have actual hands-on, in-the-trenches experience in their specific field and also been consulting for a number of years. They should have seen a number of business situations that they can apply to yours.

Beware; there are more than a few flashy, expensive consulting firms that will be happy to take your money –

just like they've taken the money of scads of corporations and deep pocketed entrepreneurs who've gone before you. They're staffed by fresh graduates who don't have the first clue about business but who went to the best schools and wear the right suits. Their business cards are first-rate. Their offices are tastefully furnished. They will bleed you dry.

You can find the former by picking up the phone and calling people you hear about who have been successful in China. You *might* find someone like that by calling your embassy, but it's doubtful. (What would government employees know about doing business?) You certainly don't want to just go online and call up the people with the most impressive website. They'll sell you before you know what's happening.

Meet with as many of the people your advisors recommend as possible, until you feel comfortable with one of them. Then and only then, should you make a hiring decision. Important: a consultant is there to advise you. Not to do your work for you. Get someone you know on the ground in China, finding out real, hard answers to your questions before you make any big decisions – preferably *this person is you.*

33. THE CHINA MARKET - 101

> AKA China isn't just a country (It's more like a whole continent)

This may be obvious to you, but I'm going to say it anyway - Don't assume just because the markets accept it at home, that it is going to fly over here.

Don't confuse Chinese markets with Western markets.

I have seen so many companies come in and try to sell to the Chinese in the same way they sell to Americans. It doesn't work.

See the next chapter for marketing tips.

And please, please, please, stop thinking of China as a single market. It's not.

You wouldn't think of Europe as a single market would you? *Would you*?

Think of Mainland China as a continent that possesses all the diversity of Europe and you'll get a good idea of how the whole culture hangs together – and separately. There's a kind of general cohesiveness, but vast differences between peoples. Officially there is only one "Chinese" language, but there are so many dialects that sound like they are different languages, your head will spin.

But wait, there's more...

There are huge differences between Mainland Chinese and those overseas: Taiwanese, Hong Kongers, and Singaporeans. As a matter of fact, Mainland Chinese are as different from Hong Kongers as Southside L.A. residents are from East-side Manhattanites in the U.S. (Psst. Mainlanders actually do NOT like to have a Hong Kong or Taiwanese boss).

If your dream is to open a café in Beijing or a cowboy bar in Shenzhen, keep this in mind. You can learn a lot from this book – but not nearly enough about your chosen market to think you can afford to skimp on more specific material.

The North is different from the South, the East coast from the West, and the first-tier cities from the third-tier, etc., etc., yada, yada, yada.

Now you know.

Do your homework.

34. YOUR 'WORLD-FAMOUS' BRAND MEANS BUPKIS HERE

AKA Yeah, but I'm huge in Germany

Imagine walking into a Chinese restaurant for the first time in your life, having never heard of a single dish on the menu. You won't know what to order. You have no idea what is considered good. You really have no cultural bearings whatsoever. There is a good chance you might not eat, unless you had an experienced friend with you.

What is traditional or famous back home may be completely new here. The good news is smaller brands can carve out a niche before the big boys come in. The bad news is the amount of marketing and educating you may have to do when you arrive.

When we first opened Beijing Sammies we had to rely on foreign students for our customer base. When they discovered how delicious our food was, they spread the word among the nationals and brought their Chinese friends with them. But we still had to spend a lot of time, energy and money educating our market through our advertising. People weren't going to come in and chow down on our sandwiches, cheesecake and cappuccino if they didn't know what they were. I mean, we're talking about a place where people aren't big risk takers with their money – not by a long shot.

Then, miracle of miracles, the big green monster (a.k.a. Starbucks) came to our rescue. They spent massive amounts of green on teaching the Chinese the immutable laws of all things coffee and pastry and convincing them that a $4 latte was something no date should be without. And plenty of those folks flooded through our doors over the next few years!

You might have a great product or service – something that will bring your Chinese customers a lot of delight or maybe even improve their lives in radical ways. But if they don't understand *what* you're selling and *why* they need it, that won't matter. Before you launch your business, ask yourself: "Am I going to have to teach my market about why they need my product?" Better yet, ask everyone you can corner in China that same question. If the answer is "yes," it's time to estimate the cost. Will you be able to do it fast enough to stay in business? What if they never buy in to your pitch? Is it worth the risk?

35. USE FACE TO SELL

AKA Mooncake Marketing

Remember: if it's not an issue of Face, then it IS an issue of price. Forget talking about quality and value.

It's not that these *don't* matter, it's that they don't matter as much as **face** and then **price**.

We have already gone over why you can't beat the Chinese on price. Don't even try and please GOD don't fool yourself.

If you think you are competing against them on quality or value, you are really going up against them on price and they will grind your face in the dirt and leave you broke, shivering and convinced you're a loser before you know what's happening. (I thought that line was worth repeating.)

Remember:
#1 Motivator is Face.
#2 Motivator is Price.

If there's a group of people anywhere in the world who would prefer to buy a Coca Cola for $15 in a fancy club before they'd buy a store-brand cola for 50 cents, it's the Chinese. At the same time, the same person, when face is

NOT an issue, will gladly go out of their way so they can wolf down a bowl of noodles for 50 cents instead of getting the same noodles at a restaurant in their building for 75 cents.

As a whole, Chinese Mainlanders who will bypass a quality product in favor of a cheap knock-off, will spend massive amounts of money on things that bring them face. Where do they get that money? Don't know. Don't care. Don't ask.

Luckily for you, exclusivity equals face, and face (being a virtual necessity) sells like you wouldn't believe. And so does the very best of the very best of anything – even if it isn't (the very best). What this means to you is you can compete with them on *face*.

Create a product or service, charge double what your closest competitor is charging and make sure that when people buy from you, the packaging will shout to everyone on the street that *you* can't afford this, but I can.

Sell face.

Let me just give you the classic example: Moon Cakes

In the 1990s the average Moon Cake cost pennies. Today, people can spend hundreds of dollars.

I for one am NOT a fan of Moon Cakes. I think the traditional moon cake tastes slightly better than cardboard and apparently has more calories than should even be possible. But we are not talking about quality remember... they are gifts.

It's about FACE yo... You're not giving Moon Cakes. YOU'RE... GIVING... FACE

So just think of the face you get when you give the Moon Cake nonchalantly, to a pal, a slinky Shanghai girl or your mother-in-law.

The kicker is the way these things are packaged. DAMN! The sparkly, glittering, gold-plated, elaborate boxes galore! (Whisper in your ear) appearance over substance...

Compared to a Moon Cake, Haagen Dazs is a bargain at twice what it costs in the West. But it's still a pricey item in a nation where workers earn a fraction of what they earn in the U.S. Only the fact that people think it's the *very best* keeps this cool dessert selling like hotcakes and providing aspiring, upwardly mobile Chinese the face they crave.

Honestly, I suspect that the right marketer could package poop in gold foil paper, slap a label on it reading "The Best Flower Fertilizer in China" and make a killing. They'd just have to charge enough for it that only the nouveau riche or politicians' families (China's version of the "Old Rich") could possibly afford it.

Sell face.

Note:
You do not need to like or agree with this practice, but if you are operating in China, you need to be aware of it and know how to use it.

Side note:
The face/price situation should NOT be confused with the situation where you watch your Chinese girlfriend arguing with a street vendor for twenty minutes insisting on paying 35 cents for a drink when the vendor tried to sell it to you for 45 cents. THAT is actually an argument about face. Your girlfriend does not want you to be cheated by someone taking advantage of the "easy target" foreigner.

Maybe she cares about you and maybe she just doesn't want to lose face by being seen with such an idiot.

36. QUALITY & VALUE?
WHO GIVES A CRAP?

I watch so many companies come in and try to sell to the China market in the same way they sell back home. Big mistake! The fact that a marketing technique works in the West does not mean it will work in China. And the fact that something sells like crazy in the West does not mean it will sell in China, either.

China's cities look and sound very westernized. But consumer tastes are still thoroughly Asian. Something we think we can't live without in the West might be completely unappealing to the folks in your Chinese target market.

Like quality and value. Two things we love, love, love in the West. And two things the Chinese really don't seem to give a hoot about.

They care about perceived quality and perceived value, but they care very little about the actual quality or value of what they're buying – at least when it comes to making their purchasing decision. Just like everybody else, they're frustrated when a new purchase tears, breaks or just plain sucks. But that's not going to affect how they spend their money in any substantive way.

The popular American restaurant chain Chili's came in a few years ago and bombed, big time. They tried to sell the Chinese a quality product at a good value, and no one was buying.

Face and price are to the growing Chinese middle-class what quality and value are to most middle-class Westerners. So Chili's was screwed before it even opened its doors.

There's no face in a trip to Chili's. It's a medium experience at a medium price. Doesn't matter how good the food is or isn't. And there are cheaper places to eat, so working- and middle- class Chinese who prefer to splurge on face and scrimp on everything else avoided it like it was salmonella central.

If you want to sell quality and value, stay home.

37. STANDARD OPERATING PRACTICE (S.O.P.) #1 — DRINK WITH THE BOYS & SING WITH THE GIRLS

If you cannot do business in China between 9:00 a.m. and 5:00 p.m., you are going to have to party.

If you are male and enjoy drinking, expect to have a great time (assuming you're smart enough NOT to make any promises or sign anything while under the influence... otherwise, look forward to an extended hangover).

If you're female, you can still have a great time. Just make sure you draw your personal boundaries before the evening starts and stick to them. Your potential partners or prospects will give you some latitude because of your gender. They won't expect you to drink as much as a man in your position.

Still, you'll have to make it clear from the first sign of trouble that you're willing to have fun and laugh with them, but you're not open to any alcohol-fueled sexual comments, gambits or advances. This will earn you their respect, and possibly even their business, as long as you are careful not to come across as judgmental of what they're doing.

So, what should you expect?

Well, it's kinda like in the movies. Consider an invitation for a night out, an initiation – because that's what it is. If you can hang with the boys, especially when it comes to alcohol consumption, you can hang with them when it comes to doing serious business – at least, that's the way your Chinese contacts are going to look at it.

FYI: The farther you get from first-tier cities, the more you have to drink.

You'll run into a couple of interesting spirits: *Ergoutou* and *Maotai*. *Ergoutou* is nasty, vile stuff. (That is just my humble opinion.) It can be bought in either $.25 bottles or 2 liter jugs, and it packs a wallop. *Maotai* is an expensive version of the same thing – a bit easier to swallow but just as hard to handle. Both come in at 60 and 90 proof. They are not for the faint of heart.

If you can, match your counterparts drink for drink. But make sure you leave your pen (or chop!) at home, along with the keys to your car. Don't make any decisions or sign any deals after 5:00. Because the odds are, if it's after 5:00, you're under the influence.

OK, so what do you do if you're on the wagon, or if you don't drink for some reason?

Well, don't simply refuse their offer of a drink with thanks. (That might make them lose face and make you look like you don't want a business relationship.)

Instead, make your excuses. Tell them you are taking medicine which prohibits you from drinking - or that you're allergic to alcohol. Say something like, "Hey, I'm up for just about anything – except for drinking!"

If you can't drink for religious reasons, simply tell them that's the case, but let them know you'll enjoy hanging out with them while they indulge. Have a joke handy to demonstrate that you're still a cool person. Then, quickly change the subject.

I still think there is a good chance they are going to find a way to get you completely drunk anyhow…

Over the course of the evening, get louder and louder, almost as though you're drinking. Make a complete fool of yourself singing "Proud Mary" or an Elvis song of your choice and, in general, keep pace with the atmosphere of fun and conviviality.

The purpose of all this partying is for your counterparts to see you when you are NOT in complete control. They are testing your character. Can they trust you? Are you like them?

So, it's your job to have a ball while you keep your wits about you OR get totally wasted and pass out so they have to take you home.

Don't lose your temper. Don't make any deals. Don't make an idiot out of yourself.

Oh yeah... the Karaoke girl thing. Hmmm... that really needs to be experienced.

Let's just say you will probably have more options than you can handle and will be expected to pay for a girl to sit beside you, drink with you and sing along. I'll leave it at that.

Oh, yeah: road rules apply. (If you need that explained to you, you are not ready for China.)

38. EVERYTHING THAT'S NOT ABOUT FACE, IS ABOUT GUANXI - II

So, if the person on the other end is not doing what you want them to, it's because they are not motivated to save face, gain/receive face or give face. (Which probably means it's become a price issue and then you are in trouble).

If you haven't been able to find the right button, this is when Guanxi comes in.

If you have not created a bond worthy of making it a face issue you are going to have to find someone who can. (This is, after all, the ultimate purpose of Guanxi)

Wait… did I just say that Guanxi is, at its core, a Face thing"?

Oh, Snap!

So it still is… ALL ABOUT FACE!

39.   YOU CAN ALWAYS
GET MORE GUANXI - II

Before you freak out or turn around to go home, don't worry. Guanxi is for sale.

Yes, you can buy yourself some Guanxi. (Come to think of it, and yet, not too surprising, you can even buy fake Guanxi.)

Guanxi is after all, the oil that greases the wheels of business.

So naturally there are Guanxi Brokers, Guanxi Consultants, Guanxi hit men, a whole host of Guanxi connections you can make. All depending which wheel needs greasing, there is a Guanxi "fixer" out there for you.

Unless you are dealing very high up or very specific, BEWARE of the "one-size-fits-all" Guanxi tool.

There are a number of snake-oil Guanxi salesmen out there that will fill your head with names of "good buddies" (*tie ge'mer*) and waste your time and money with unfulfilled promises.

They are experienced con men, always dangling a carrot in front of you and quick with excuses.

They may even ask for no payment while they are working. They, will however, ask for expenses or they may introduce you to a few connections along the way.

Just like any other job you're filling, get references.
Remember, Guanxi is NOT something mystical or magical. Guanxi is something you may not currently have, but think of it as a business connection and deal with it like you would normally deal with a business hurdle: objectively and professionally (as opposed to leaving your common sense outside).

40. "THAT'S A GREAT IDEA! THANKS!"

China wants your money, your knowledge, your experience, your talent, your technology, and anything else you've got rattling around in your brain. But it doesn't want to pay you for it.

DEAL WITH IT.

The truth is, the Chinese place almost no financial value on intellectual property or copyrights, in large part because of the communist ideologies in which they've been immersed since their earliest childhood. Learn by rote. Do as you are told. Follow the company rules. Copy. Copy. Copy.

If you are successful and I follow you, my risk of making a mistake and therefore losing face is low. Why do something new or different? It's just too risky.

You can expect knock-offs and outright, in-the-open idea and information theft because, for the most part, no one will stop you.

Not too long ago, a couple of guys set up a Facebook knock-off, sold it to some people, and then turned around and set up another Facebook knock-off.

And they're getting away with it, my friend.

Protect your trade secrets, your plans and your creative ideas like they're vital to your security – because they are. (Your financial security, anyway!)

And this brings us to a discussion of an extremely powerful mindset that will impact your business life at least once – and probably many times – over the course of your business life in China.

41. IF YOU GET CONNED, YOU HAD IT COMING

This belief pervades much of the Chinese business environment.

In the U.S., if you get taken on a deal, you might get a lot of sympathy – and maybe even a great deal of help from the authorities. In China, if you get taken on a deal, you might want to keep it under wraps. You're unlikely to get much sympathy (especially as a "rich foreigner"). And you're even less likely to get any real help from the police – or the legal system.

It was about a month after Beijing Sammies opened and we were going gangbusters, when I flew back to Toronto for my sister's wedding. When I got back, my partner said "Sam, we've got a problem."

It turned out that the guy who'd rented us our restaurant space had taken the six months' rent we'd paid him and lit out of town. The street committee had waited for their money, ran out of patience, and finally showed up at our door to demand their dough.

They didn't care, of course, that we'd paid our rent: "We can't find him, but we can find you. Where's **our** money? Hand it over."
We handed it over.

Please note that it is NOT that the Chinese are out to screw over foreigners. It is simply easier to screw over foreigners. The business environment over here can be harsh even to other Chinese.

You've been warned.

If anything, people will look at you as being foolish.
If you were stupid enough to get conned, it's because YOU... WERE... STUPID... ENOUGH.... TO... GET... CONNED.

See where this is going?

Move on and NO WHINING!

OK...OK...Don't step in the following common traps...

1. The Tea Ceremony

You're new in town, walking down the street thinking about how your cousin Jake is a total loser for selling his soul to corporate America when a sweet little child engages you in conversation and then (wonder of wonders!) invites you to a genuine tea ceremony. You have a delightful time, soaking up the culture – until her mother hands you a bill for $100. You've just been had – a victim of the infamous tea ceremony scam.

Similar to the art exhibition scam.

Buying a pretty girl a drink in a bar

You're relaxing at a bar when a beautiful young woman wanders over to you, asks you if you're a foreigner, and then begs prettily to practice her English with you. Before you know it, you're buying her a drink. Of course, you have no clue that her drinks are costing you four times what they'd go for back home.

After a couple of hours, you get hit with a $200 bar tab. You're not going to pay it! You refuse! But you change your mind quickly when her "brother" Chang and his friends surround you with menacing looks and no escape in sight. You decide discretion is the better part of valor, ante up the dough, and vow never to return to that particular pub.

3. Tourist traps

You may be lucky enough not to get caught by either of those scams, but you won't be able to avoid this last one. Well, it's not so much a scam as a... well, okay, it's a scam.

Here, every time you go to a tourist trap, they not only *hope* you'll buy a souvenir; they *expect* you to buy one. The tour guides get commissions for the souvenirs their "guides" purchase – and they're perfectly willing to pressure, harass and (failing those!) glower at you until you open your wallet and do the right thing.

117

In their eyes, you're the "rich foreigner," and to you, you're thinking, "Oh come on, it only costs xyz and means so much to them and so little to me"... right?

Don't sweat the small stuff. Do what feels right and then don't ever fall into the conversation on how much you paid, because you probably did overpay, but it's such a little bit of money and means so little to you and so much to them...

Before you come, do a web search on scams, fraud etc. It's worth the time to read about it.

42. GET A LAWYER, BUT DON'T COUNT ON THE LAW

You will never understand Chinese law, much less Chinese law in your industry. Find a local lawyer who specializes in licensing and other legal requirements for businesses like yours. Choose someone with Guanxi – someone you trust, someone who has references from other entrepreneurs. (And call them before you pay your retainer!)

Make sure you and your lawyer communicate well and easily. There can be no room for error when your fortune's at stake.

That being said... don't count on the law to resolve business conflicts for you. In China, the law is a last resort or no resort at all for companies at war with each other.

An agreement that suffers from bad faith (on one or both sides) or from misunderstandings is not likely to end up in court, it's more likely to end up in anger and resentment – with no clear resolution.

The scenario changes a bit when a foreigner is at the helm of the "opposing" company. In that case, the Mainlander concerned might decide to take their chances on a legal system notorious for its prejudice against foreigners.

I have heard of one case in which a ruling went in favor of a foreign company over a local corporation. The foreign company won the case, but they never could collect damages.

43.   BEIJING SAMMIES – 1st SIX MONTHS

In addition to pretending to be an architect, interior designer, baker and restauranteur, I then did a little improvisation when it came to hiring the first crew.

The year before, I had gone to the first Subway subs to open in China. You know, for a little recon. I was struck by one of their assistant managers and how diligently she took her job. In my rudimentary Chinese I told her I was thinking about starting my own café and would like to hire her to manage it.

She smiled at me and said she would be interested to talk further when I was closer to getting it off the ground. She was a few years older than me, already married with a kid, so not going to quit her stable job for a promotion in a dream.

I visited her a number of times before we found the location. When we started renovations, she informed me that her husband was currently out of a job and I could hire him to start. So I did. He became the first Beijing Sammies employee.

I remember interviewing a number of people before we opened. No one knew what a sandwich was, or a cappuccino or a smoothie.

I remember one lady coming in and with heavily made-up doe-like eyes telling me she was a really good drinker.

Pause… "I'm sorry, what did you say? You are really good drinker….?"

*3…2…1… OH! You are a karaoke girl and you think a café is a bar. You think I am opening a **bar**!!!! Now, I get it. You just have to tell me 2-3 times and then I understand.*

I put a crew together, went to Silk Alley to buy everyone matching shirts and plain blue baseball hats and then taught them the fine art of making sandwiches.

When we started we ordered our bread from the ONLY bread supplier in the city. (There was actually a lady in Beijing who made bagels, but she wanted to charge retail prices (about 75 cents/bagel). I told her my customers were students and couldn't afford the high prices, but she wouldn't budge. I vowed to get back at her.) I remember days when they didn't deliver the bread until 12:30. There were almost fights. But what could we do? We were a small potato and they were the only supplier.

Before I began, I thought I would be able to outsource quite a bit, but as soon as the wheels were in motion, I realized we would have to do a lot ourselves. We became our own bakery and made our own cookies, muffins and brownies.

It was probably the third week of operations that the need to create systems came to me. I was tired of making all the baked goods. I asked who was interested in baking, Two girls said "yes" and the next time I made brownies, they watched and took notes. The next day with me watching, one made brownies in the morning the other in the afternoon. By Day Three they were on their own and I began systemizing the café.

We had the BEST sandwiches, the BEST smoothies, the BEST coffee, and the BEST desserts within miles of the school.

We broke even in our second month, paid off the cash register, the air conditioner and the even our Sammies sign. Each week we got better and better. In fact, the assistant manager from Subway came on board in Month Three. By the time I went back to Canada for my sister's wedding, things were looking really, really good.

Yes, here it comes...

As soon as I returned, there were signs of trouble, i.e. my partner was coming by more often. I believe the appropriate term would be "casing the joint," but in an overt, business way.

Within 24 hours of returning, the street committee [†] comes knocking on our door, looking for their rent from the past six months[‡]. Yeah, the first landlord had done a runner.

We were shocked to hear about the situation, and while we said we had paid the rent, the street committee's response was a simple, "Well, we can't find him, but we can find you. Pay us or go."

Oh %*#@.

Arguing with the government? – Hmmm...not a good idea.

I was beyond angry at my partner. This was his ONE responsibility. Why didn't you take care of this? Up and down I yelled. I had invested everything and had been working my butt off getting the café working and now this could possibly muck everything up.

I told him he'd better take care of it and fast!

The next night, I was awakened at 4:30 a.m. by the security guard we had hired the day before (his job was basically, to sleep over every night). My "partner" had

---

[†] The street committee is like the lowest rung on the government ladder
[‡] Two months of renovations and almost four months of operating

come in the middle of the night, stolen the partially finished licenses and kicked the security guard out.

Sammies was doing well. All of the staff were already trained. Everything was already in his name, so why not take over the café?

I jumped on my bike (come on, I was a student a few months earlier and it was China... you think I had a car?), and rode over to the café. As I pulled the door open, the lock completely splintered. I guess my partner had changed the locks, but since he was drinking, he didn't do such a good job. (Either that, or my adrenalin filled body was powerful as to...yeah right.)

So he wanted the café huh? Well he could have it. But I was going to take out everything in it. I bought it all, it was mine.

Luckily, earlier the previous day I had mentioned to a friend who owned a hotel nearby, that I may need some of his help very, very soon. So at 5:00 a.m. I called him up and he sent over a bus and some of his guards. Within two hours, we had cleaned out the entire café, including the kitchen sink, and moved it all over to his hotel. I thanked everyone and told them there would be no more work for the rest of the day.

I am sure my partner was expecting me to call him

around 8:00 a.m., when the morning shift couldn't get in. I got a call from him at 9:00 p.m.

"So what do you want to do?" he asks me.

"What do YOU want to do? You can have the café, but the stuff is mine."

Silence....

"Let's meet tomorrow to discuss," he says.

Excellent.

Here's what happened....

I went back to my old dorm and asked this Russian who was built like a brick-shit-house to sit at a table beside us while we talked. First with his back to us, so we were back to back, and then 30 minutes later to sit on the other side of his table thereby facing our table and facing my partner.

Before opening the café I was dating a Russian girl (she was 1/4 Chinese and just beautiful) and I told my soon-to-be-ex-partner that some of the funding for the café came from what could be described as the Russian mafia. That was a complete lie, but he didn't know this. I also told him that "they" were pleased with how well we had done in such a short period of time and would like me to continue.

If he would like to operate a café in our original spot, a spot they were very familiar with, then he could go right ahead. I would take the equipment and move somewhere else.

It was about this time that the Brick-Shit-House moved to the other side of the table and started staring menacingly at my soon-to-be-ex-partner.

Strangely enough he decided to not become a restaurateur and requested some funds to get out of the way. I gave him a tiny portion of it and told him to never bother me again.

In less than ten days of the takeover attempt, Sammies was open again for business. Unfortunately my negotiations were not finished. The street committee[§] had not been placated.

I told them we would pay the previous six months again, but we want to then be the first level renter. (You see, the street committee had rented to the first guy who in turn rented to us.) Basically, we had paid double the initial

---

[§] Two months of renovations and almost four months of operating

amount. In the long term, it would be a cheaper amount (as if I had any real bargaining leverage).

They said OK, give us the money.

I paid the money and 2 days later a new guy knocks on the door and says he's the new landlord and he wants us out. Yes, I was foolish enough to believe them and didn't get it in writing first. That new landlord ended up renting the location to us for pretty much the same amount as the first landlord.

Basically, somebody in the street committee gave the rights to a buddy and probably split the profits. But, by the time the new school year had begun, everything was back to normal.

Section IV

Negotiating with the Dragon

You have to be prepared that at the end of the day, they do just want to eat you up.

44.   PICK YOUR PARTNERS WELL

I know very few people who have not been screwed over by a Chinese partner. Okay, I know one person who hasn't been screwed over by a Chinese partner.

I do not think it is as simple as thinking foreigners have an almost fool-proof ability to glide past those salt-of-the-earth Chinese who deserve our trust and head right for the fast-talking, charismatic types who target us for exploitation. It's never that cut and dry.

A psychologist recently told me that people who are in the midst of a major life transition tend to fall in love much more rapidly than other folks. Apparently, a heightened sense of insecurity both compromises the executive functions of the brain (i.e. good judgment!) and facilitates bonding. Certainly the lure of the potential, the excitement of the deal and the desire to get going affect our choices.

When it comes to finding the right partner, Mom's words still apply: "Don't take candy from strangers." At the same time, don't take candy from friends just because they offer it.

I chose my first partner for Beijing Sammies in large part because he was my best friend's cousin and seemed like a great guy. It was a nightmare of a business relationship.

Plenty of Chinese warned me this would be the case.

"Listen, Sam," my future coffee supplier said one day, "if you do well, you've got 6-8 months before your partner tries to screw you over."

"He's my best friend's cousin!" I protested.

"Exactly."

And he was almost right. It was four months before he screwed me over.

I don't beat myself up about it because, for one thing, I was very young and therefore excusably stupid. But the truth is people of all ages and experience levels tend to form partnerships based on interpersonal factors like that. It's a very human thing to do.

If you decide to go into partnership with someone, do your due diligence.

Get to know them as well as you can on a personal level. Make opportunities to talk with people who know them and dig (discreetly or otherwise) for information on their character and honesty.

A good, thorough background check is more than a good idea. It's a necessity.

And don't stop there. Find out how "hands-off" they're likely to remain once things start heating up in the business.

Most of all, give the negotiation process time to expose ulterior motives or bad habits before you sign on the dotted line.

Most important: listen to your instincts. A potential partner may *look* great, *talk* great and *seem* great. But if your gut just won't stop nagging at you, if you just can't feel comfortable about doing business with them, don't.

Go with your gut.

45. A GOOD CONTRACT IS A GOOD... BEGINNING!

AKA How you should view a contract.

I hope you have heard this before. But just in case... contracts in China are, for the most part, just a new chapter in your ongoing relationship.

Think of your contract like you would wedding vows. At the time of making the vows you either meant them, or knew flat-out that the words were hollow. And you also knew that, in this day and age (unfortunately), no one would actually hold you to keeping them.

A marriage is like any relationship; it takes work. Well, in China, your work relationship is like a marriage.

Westerners tend to work hard at the beginning of a relationship to work out a solid contract, so everyone has a roadmap on expectations moving forward.

Breaking a contract is wrong and although renegotiations happen, they don't happen at the drop of a hat.

Not so much here.

Everything you agree to in the contract that is in their favor (like time schedules and prices), you can be sure they will hold your feet to the fire on it. Stuff that is in your favor that they find difficult to adhere to (like time schedules and prices), well, you may find yourself discussing them again.

If there are penalties involved... you're not seriously going to risk souring the "relationship" just for over a week's delay or a few extra dollars are you?

The answer is *of course not...* but (repeat after me) someone in the back office, someone you have *no control* over is sticking to the letter of the contract and there is "nothing you can do about it."

Don't expect them to just back down, you may eventually give in, but only after they have to give in for something too.

In China, a contract is a way to show you're serious about doing business with someone. It shows that you're creating a business relationship. It's certainly not something you'll ever want to count on – or present to a judge with a self-righteous flourish.

In America, "a deal's a deal." The Chinese operate according to an entirely different "contract economy" which sees the contract as a *sign* of good faith. Here, a contract is one piece of a very large puzzle – rather than the puzzle, itself. This is not a matter of integrity. It's a matter of *perspective.*

For inexperienced Westerners doing business in China, it's easy to sign a contract and think it means you have a deal while the people on the other side of the negotiation think it just means you're all getting along famously. And as relationship-focused people, they have no hesitancy about re-negotiating with people with whom they're getting along famously. This is just one of the ways Westerners get screwed by our own cultural contract ineptitude time and time again in China.

I remember one contract clause I worked on for the Western side, a condition termed as a "firm and fixed", price, i.e. you do *that* work and we are going to give you *that* much. The Western side interpreted this as the maximum they were going to spend and the Chinese side saw it as the minimum amount they would receive. Of course each side was happy, but for different reasons.

That was caught early on; I remember when the construction team quit in the middle of renovations for the first Beijing Sammies. They just decided I wasn't paying them enough and walked off the job. Oh, no! What was I going to do?

I was going to pay them more money, of course, or end up with a half-finished restaurant. So, I scrambled and came up with enough to meet their demands. And they came back to work smiling and laughing with me as though they hadn't just held a gun to my head days before. Because really, screwing me hadn't been their intention at all.

What can you do? You can lessen the impact of this cultural reality by tying contractors' and vendors' compensation to clear, measurable performance objectives from the very start. It won't turn your contracts into iron-clad agreements, but it will be a good clarification tool. It will help you avoid at least some of the follow-up haggling that will inevitably occur.

46.   S.O.P. #2 – GETTING YOU
ON THE BOAT

If you get into a negotiation and everything runs smoothly.

Be afraid…Be very afraid.

S.O.P #2 translates into, "Just do whatever it takes to get you on the boat."

Because once the boat sets sail and you are on board, what are you going to do, jump ship?

Think about it… You've negotiated the Letter of Intent. Head office is happy. Money, technology, whatever, is ready to be invested and the venture begins.

Well once a commitment is made or money is spent or the technology is transferred, your value has decreased considerably. In fact, you may not even be needed anymore.

This is when the negotiations REALLY start or the cabin crew starts asking for more money or they just get downright unfriendly and wait for you to leave.

47. DON'T LET HOSPITALITY TAKE YOU HOSTAGE

I like to call it "social debt." Your sparring partner in an important negotiation treats you to a lovely dinner, flies you out to their comfortable corporate retreat, or puts you up in a gorgeous suite. They procure a command performance for you, work hard to entertain and pamper you. Or they simply welcome you warmly, show you to a comfortable seat, and give you a delicious, cool drink. Regardless of how extravagant or modest their efforts are, one thing is clear: in any mainland Chinese negotiation, the ultimate goal of hospitality is to make you comfortable so they can make you uncomfortable about standing your ground and refusing a low-ball offer or giving up things you wouldn't give up if you were on your own turf.

So, what can you do to counter this tactic or use it to your advantage? You can be effusive with your thanks and your ground anyway. You can ensure you're never in the "one down" position to start with, by arranging to meet on your home turf, or in a neutral place where neither of you or your companies will be "host." You can even use their hospitality as a justification for making a concession you want to make anyway.

But what you should never do is let the fact that your sparring partner's executive assistant brought you a bottle of Evian and a crystal glass after seating you in the most comfortable chair in the room lull you into giving up something you weren't already prepared to give up when you walked in.

48. SMILE, THEY'RE OUT TO SCREW YOU

You think I'm being cynical?

Well, what's the worst that will happen if you think like this?

You'll be pleasantly surprised.

The best?

You won't be frozen with shock when it happens.

To be forewarned is to be forearmed.

49. STAYING POWER

Remember the Chinese Water Torture? Well, for really big negotiations, the Chinese side's #1 tactic is to wear you down.

Be advised, they are very, very experienced on doing this.

First they butter you up.

Then they will smile a lot, drag their feet all the while you think you are making progress and things are going well. You will be the hamster running on the wheel.

Then, when you start to get tired, they bring in some new people, a new boss, or some more engineers. They will put you through the same paces, but this time the niceties will be shorter and by the end of it, they are pummeling you. First with big ole' over-sized Nerf gloves, but day after day, week after week, the gloves become smaller and the pummeling gets tougher.

Your initial contact, your "friends" who brought you in to this, will show up every once in a while to check in, smile a lot and "see what they can do to help you out."

After they have thoroughly worn you down and after you have spent way more time and money than you thought you would, then they will show you the light at the end of the tunnel.

They **will** continue to bring up issues you thought were closed.

People on their side **will** ask for some *CRAZY* things

(There is no harm in asking and you just might be stupid enough to agree to one or two)

So what are you going to do about all this?

Knowing ahead of time hopefully will avoid a lot of it, but when you do find yourself getting worn down, TAKE A BREAK!

Tell them you are needed back home on urgent matters. Tell them you have to write a report for a superior or board member and will be back in a week.

Avoid meeting over the weekends and use the Monday for your team to regroup. Don't use the weekend to go over more stuff and hit the Monday without ever getting some time off. Sure you can do this on the first weekend and maybe the second weekend, but by the end of the third week, you are operating at very low efficiency levels. Brain. Stops. Functioning.

If your goal becomes to just close the deal, then the real pain is just beginning.

Quick note about professional negotiators or business development types: You absolutely want to have someone on the negotiation team who is going to be responsible for implementing the deal. China can't be a short term play, but for those whose main responsibility is to close the deal, that is exactly what China is.

So when your team is knee deep in crap that could have been avoided, your business development person is off somewhere else closing another deal.

50. SIZE MATTERS

There is strength in numbers. That's why you may arrive for what you think is a simple or low-level negotiation and find yourself sitting across a giant conference table, with six or eight people lined up on the other side. They will look important. They will be self-contained and authoritative. They may be window-dressing.

Here's the scoop: Chinese negotiators will have as many people come to a negotiation session as they can gather, simply to create an impressive or even intimidating presence. For this purpose, it doesn't matter a hoot whether all (or even most!) of the folks on their side of the table have a clue about what's going on in the meeting. They're there to outnumber you, for the psychological advantage it will give the person (or people) with the real influence and power.

As a matter of fact, a lot of Chinese deal-makers are perfectly happy to dress their janitor in a suit, call in the part-time receptionist and get the president's irresponsible, pot-head little brother to put on a tie and drag himself into the office for the afternoon if it means they'll have more people staring you down in a meeting. I'm only slightly exaggerating here.

All that being said, you can do the same. Pack your side of the table with people from your company, if you're representing a corporation and have the man (and woman!) power to do it. Failing that, convince your racquet-ball buddy, your wife, your father-in-law and your unemployed friend from the gym to suit up and show up for the meeting as your "team."

You don't have to make up titles for them. Simply describe them as your team members and introduce them by name. Tell them ahead of time to keep their mouths closed, look serious, frown often, and take lots of notes. And then encourage them to gossip with the opposing side during breaks, in case they can glean information that will help you size up or out-negotiate them.

Once, while I was consulting with a Canadian investment firm, my client and I decided he should not introduce me, so that I could be a "non-person" throughout the meeting, gathering information to which I would not be privy – if the opposing team had understood my actual role as an advisor. Because my position was not known the opposing side spoke freely, as if a child with no understanding were in the room.

In practice, you will often find yourself facing a person or people with no idea as to their genuine roles, power or influence. Don't make the mistake of under-estimating them. (And warn your junior team members not to spill your business secrets during breaks!)

51.   HOME COURT ADVANTAGE - I

Make every effort to meet on neutral turf.

Chinese business people like to invite you to negotiate with them on their home turf for several reasons. But, one of the most important reasons to keep in mind is convenience. By that, I mean *their* convenience.

Westerns tend to try to get a deal done on a timeline. You will want to make your flight home to the U.S. or back to Shanghai two weeks from now. By playing on their turf they have the luxury of carrying on business-as-usual in their offices when they're not meeting with you. Who do you think is going to have the upper hand?

It's not unusual for a negotiation predicted to last two weeks to drag on for a month, or two... or even longer. You can easily find yourself working twelve or fourteen hours a day, six or seven days a week - and don't forget, they probably have more human resources to throw into this than you do.

You will be away from your family and friends. You will get sick of living at a hotel, missing whatever life you had and you will find yourself just wanting the frickin' negotiations to be DONE!

Asking to have half the negotiations on your turf will probably be used against you. Be aware that it will almost certainly be difficult for their team to get visas to visit your country (something they are well aware of and may use to their advantage. Heck, after they tell you this, you may even feel a bit *embarrassed* for asking. Don't get sucked in.) Before you make this rookie mistake and before you get worn down - be prepared to take breaks.

Even make them part of your unwritten game plan. If everyone knows walking in to the fray that there is a break day at the end of every XXth day then psychologically they will not feel as burnt out. Remember, plowing through negotiations just to get them done is only going to come back and haunt you later.

52.   THE SILENT TREATMENT

Get comfortable, right now, with the idea of enduring silence during negotiations. I'm not talking about silence after meetings, while they leave you dangling and wondering about decisions for weeks or months at a time (though they'll often do that, too!). I'm talking about genuine,   scary,   no-one-is-talking-and-it-has-been-at-least-three-minutes silences that will happen right in the middle of discussions.

They will often happen after you have quoted a price or established a condition.

The first one to talk loses.

This is passivity as a power play, and it works when they use it on emotional Westerners, 9 times out of 10.

53. HOME COURT ADVANTAGE - II

You do not want the prevailing law to be in the PRC.

The other side will, of course, demand it.

And as much as *you* would to accommodate them (*wink wink*), you will (repeat after me) unfortunately be unable to concede because someone on your Board (people not in the room) will not allow it.

Or better yet, tell them that should be OK, but you will have to pass this by the Board first; passing over that issue until later.

Any experienced lawyer worth their salt will find a way to structure the deal so the law is in neutral territory.

54.   DETERMINE THE DECISION MAKER(S)

In any business dealing, you want to determine the decision maker as soon as possible.

In China, Westerners often spend weeks or months hammering out a deal only to discover that the person or team they've been working with is virtually powerless – simply presenting a united front, gathering information, and reporting all they see and hear to the guy or gal in the corner office who has the "go or no" authority.

One word from the officer who's really in charge, and you're either in the money or out of luck. So, you want to find out who they are - and do everything you can to deal with them, directly.

You will often find the person you were supposed to meet with gets called away to some other urgent matter, leaving you sitting with a junior team whose sole purpose is to wear you down. The performance of these guys will in fact be measured by how much time they spend with you, the concessions they make from you etc.

One of their favorite tricks is to line up meetings with engineers who can't commit to anything on their end, but are there to ask you questions, request further clarification, give you problems to solve, and generally get something from you for free. When this happens, know what you can talk about and what you can't.

Politely say, "Sorry, we are not prepared to talk about that right now". Then let them know what you need before you can continue and repeat the steps as often as they require you to do so.

55.   ACHIEVE PROGRESSION BY CONCESSION

Always go into a negotiation situation ready to give something up. Consider yourself the savvy virgin who is never, ever, ever going to put out for her boyfriend – but who will eventually allow herself to be coaxed into handing over a French kiss or two. The key word is "eventually."

Believe me, they've come in prepared for you to bargain hard. They're happy to shoot for the moon and settle for the Empire State Building.

You've got to prove them right if you want to keep their respect. Sure, they'll pitch you for gigantic concessions and act like they expect you to bend over and take it. But really, they're just seeing if you'll be stupid enough to agree. It's a win-win for them. If you agree, they're ahead. If you don't? Well, they haven't really lost anything, and by setting the bar higher than it would have been otherwise, they've come across as making a kind of concession, themselves.

You'll be totally shocked at how often you can take a big, crazy "I cannot effing believe they just asked me for that with a straight face" demand with a simple concession.

So what are you going to do? Politely and quickly dismiss the outlandish requests as not part of this deal, something you would be willing to discuss later as a separate deal or something that would have to be reviewed first by people not in the room and therefore not up for discussion right now.

You can also prepare some dummy requests of your own as well as frame small issues as bigger than they are. Then when you do give them up, you are getting real value for them. I will assume that you have already read a number of books on negotiating, so will not go over that here. You may also want to check out my version of the classic 36 Stratagems at www.where-east-eats-west.com for a number of tactics that the Chinese side is probably already well aware of.

56. YOUR HAPPINESS = THEIR LOSS OF FACE

Westerners go into negotiations and strive for that "win-win" contract. Chinese on the other hand, give that lip service when it is in their favor, but deep down, they don't believe there's such thing as "win-win."

If you are happy with a result and they can see that you're happy, it means they gave you too much. This means they did not negotiate hard enough and their boss will not be happy which will make them lose face.

Never forget, in the minds of most Chinese negotiators, if there is a winner, then there must be a loser

In the West we use enthusiasm to cement a warm working relationship. Curb your enthusiasm. Put your poker face on. Talk up small things as if they were big things, so when you concede to one them, they will think they got more than they did.

In China, expressions of enthusiasm can make them think they've been had. Why would you be so happy if you hadn't just figured out a way to screw them, after all?

57. REFUSE TO PLAY THE SHAME GAME

AKA Pack your bags, we're going on a guilt trip.

China's 5000 year history is full of foreigners coming in, taking advantage of poor-hapless Chinese. They've got shame, and they're not afraid to use it.

Yes, shame is a favorite Chinese negotiating tactic. They'll exploit your mistakes – or even convince you that you've made mistakes when you haven't. They'll question your good faith, imply that your motives are impure, and play the "offended" card when they're nothing of the sort – all to put you at a disadvantage.

Their accusations may be implied or stated outright:

"Aren't we friends?"

"You've violated our trust."

"This is not a sign of good faith."

"Don't you trust that we are acting in good faith?"

Don't argue. Make a small gesture of good will. One small gesture of good will can turn the tables back in your favor.

Most of all, stick to your guns.

58.   USE FACE IN YOUR FAVOR

So, you're sitting across the table from a row of poker-faced negotiators, and they're not about to budge on a "make-or-break" issue for you. They won't lower their price to one you can possibly afford to pay. Or they won't pay the price you need in order to make a profit. Or... whatever.

Use face to your advantage. Face they will gain, or lose if/when...

Indirectly offer them something of "face value," by making some of your arguments, connecting their agreement to your terms, to their gaining or losing face.

"Have you seen the incredible quality of (insert their top competitor's name here) brochures? It is too bad you will have to use the lower-quality paper. But that is the only kind of paper I could use at the price you have stated."

This allows you to put more on the table, without actually having to put *more* on the table.

59. THE BIG, GIGANTIC, ENORMOUS CARROT IN THE SKY

Chinese negotiators will often try to use the promise of a lucrative, long-term relationship to wrangle concessions out of naïve Westerners – or even persuade you take losses on a deal, because the *next* stage is where the real money comes in, or this stage is just to "learn" (in which case, after they have learned, your value will be what???)

If anything, it should be your side that is painting the picture of what is to come. You should be coming in with a game plan that extends beyond this negotiation. If you cannot communicate the even bigger pot of gold after this step, your value is short lived.

And do not think they can see it if you haven't spelled it out to them.

And make sure the decision makers you are talking to can see clearly what the value of this deal and the next is, for THEM.

60. THEY'RE USING YOU TO GET TO YOUR SISTER

How many Western corporate types and entrepreneurs have engaged in weeks or months of negotiations with a Chinese company, only to find out that the company has been using them as leverage to get a better deal with a competitor the whole time?

Expect concurrent competition

61. WHAT DO YOU MEAN I'M THE MISTRESS?

AKA Undercover Entrepreneurs

How many Western corporate types and entrepreneurs have become 'hitched' to a Chinese company, only to find out months later, that the company has been cheating on them with at least one competitor the whole time?

Odds are good that if your business is a success, you'll be a victim of what I call an "undercover entrepreneur." All your corporate secrets (your pillow talk) is being shared with unseen competition. They may be starting two companies at the same time or they are using your company as a testing ground. Once they have learned all they want, they up and leave, setting up shop next door doing the exact same thing, but this time for 30% cheaper.

I know of a half dozen stories of employees who, after learning the ropes, go off to start their own competing business. I know this happens everywhere. If it happens where you live it usually sounds like this.

The break is friendly with the competing business operating far enough away as to not, at least not immediately, be direct competition.

Or the break is nasty, in which case the animosity is pretty obvious or well known.

In China, things tend to work a little differently (the pain feels more acute).

Sammies Moment:
Kallie (not her real name; not to protect the innocent, because she was really a backstabbing witch, but I digress...) was introduced to me by a friend when I was in need of a new executive assistant as a mature, hard worker. The timing was perfect and she really was an excellent addition to the Sammies team. We worked well together for over a year before she started to ask me if she could try something different, a position in Sales.

As pleasant and good a worker as Kallie was, she had not shown the tenacity and the ability to pick herself up after rejection that sales people have to possess. I knew she wanted to learn more, but I was sure a position in Sales would mean the end of Kallie, because should she fail at Sales, she'd be too proud to come back to her current position.

A few months later, the position for the corporate Catering Manager was available and I asked if Kallie would consider that positionas an opportunity for growth. The corporate catering business was more customer service and logistics with the customers coming to us whereas the sales position was going out to new companies to build corporate sales. Her organizational skills and maturity fit better with this customer-oriented environment and the management position gave her the ability to learn even more.

She was overjoyed, was given the month of training and studied very well. Things went OK for a few months. She began to get her management legs and started to understand the how to delegate tasks and motivate her small staff (3 customer service and 10 delivery boys).

March 2003 was the best month ever for Sammies, breaking records throughout the company. In April 2003, we were hit by the SARS train which totally derailed the entire company (not to mention the city).

Corporate catering stayed busy, but instead of the average 20-person orders we got for lunch meetings, we got 20 single orders all over the city. People were not going to work and large meeting were just not happening. This continued for about two months. (Overall sales plummeted by 80% – devouring our cash reserves)

All bets were off for the monthly sales goals and many staff went on requested holidays at a fraction of their normal wage. Kallie, like the rest of the managers, suffered during the SARS time.

Business started to pick back up around the summer time, but it was as if the company itself was struck with SARS and we were recovering slowly. SARS was around for about two months but its effects lasted 6-8 months.

I had planned to bring in a new Operations Manager, but SARS wiped that plan out and by the time the summer was over, I was exhausted.

I went on vacation during the October Golden Week which was the week when Kallie quit.

I was completely surprised. She had planned to take a vacation the end of October, which would have meant, with the Golden Week holiday, she would be at the company only one more week before leaving. Not really much time to find and train a replacement. I called her up to find out why she quit as well as ask her to cancel her vacation in lieu of payment; we needed her to be there to transfer the position.

The next day two of the three Customer Service girls quit too.

This was really, really bad, not to mention fishy.

Waiting till the boss was away to do all this is not uncommon; an avoiding confrontation sort of thing, not to mention that it completely trashed my vacation.

I called back to HR and asked her what the hell was going on over there and she told me, "It's nuts."

I'm thinking, *come on, this is Kallie. I've worked with her for almost 2 years...*

Then, I find out that the third Customer Service girl had actually quit two weeks earlier, but Kallie had never told the HR manager.

Kallie gave me the story that one of the delivery boys had threatened her and she just wanted a break from working because SARS had taken a lot out of her too.

Well, I returned after a less than relaxing trip to what was to be my Black Monday, finding out Kallie didn't quit because of any threats, but because she was going to open a new business. She took the two Customer Service girls, some delivery boys, a few production staff, our customer database and some equipment to open-surprise, surprise: Kallie's Delivery.

It was like being stabbed in the back.

62. BYOT: BRING YOUR OWN TRANSLATOR

Unless someone on your team has really, really good Chinese, get a translator.

You think you're saying you want to buy a horse. Your Chinese listener hears you saying you want to sell your mother.

Don't use the translator they offer you, if you can avoid it. Get the best translator you can afford. Get one that has experience in your industry (thereby knowing all your industry jargon) and has actually done negotiations before. You'll also want to make sure to ask if she has ever worked for the other side.

Important: The only time you want to choose your translator based on her looks is when the other party speaks English very well.

63. IGNORANCE IS NOT BLISS

AKA Beware of 'Unseen Guanxi'

The fact is, just about every business deal in China is built on Guanxi, or some sort of relationship. What does this mean for you? It means that if you succeed in building a strong relationship, it should only get better and more lucrative with time. It also means you may very well have to accommodate a company's *existing* (known or unknown) Guanxi to seal any given deal.

I worked for a firm that went through the bidding process for a major account; it was courted by two sub-suppliers – each vying for the same subcontract on the project we were pitching. One sub-supplier had a proven track record doing exactly what we needed them to do for our potential customer. The other did not. They were a newly formed company, untried at projects like the one we were trying to sell, and we considered them far too big a risk to take – especially when we had such a proven alternative. This company was also an extension of another company we had other contracts with.

So, we awarded the contract to the proven sub-supplier. Shortly thereafter, the customer called us in to begin discussions on another aspect of the other contract and maybe continue to discuss the contract recently awarded to the other company. After three days of listening to them discuss why the new company was qualified to earn the contract, the customer called us into a side room to let us know that they would not let us choose the experienced company and we would in fact CHOOSE the newly formed company to get this part of the deal done. In fact, the customer had already called the other company to let them know that they would not get the contract (before they informed us).

As it turned out, having a long-standing relationship with the firm was more important than experience. They'd expected us to discover this through our research and take the hint. When we didn't, they got tough.

And we got in line.

Side note:
I am sure the company that was passed over would eventually be compensated with another project, so as to avoid too much face being lost.

64. WHEN NECESSARY, GET ANGRY

When did we all become such pansies? I gotta tell you: way too many Westerners check their balls at the door when they negotiate with the Chinese. They've read book after book warning them about a thousand and one ways you can offend the Chinese, and they're all tied up in knots, scared they're going to forget one and screw things up but good.

The party most afraid of offending is, automatically, the subordinate party. It's the party set up to lose. Don't believe for a moment that a savvy Chinese negotiator won't use your sensitivity about offending your Asian counterparts to their advantage.

Don't get me wrong; repeat offenders, people with ongoing anger problems, eventually wear out their welcome, of course. But for most part, an occasional "venting" is not only allowed but seen as a sign of good faith and openness. Just as in the West, passion can be a plus. At best, an emotional, even angry response can be viewed as a sign of honesty and commitment. At worst, it can be forgiven with an apology. If you should genuinely offend someone during a negotiation, a simple apology will go a lot further than it normally would in a Westerner-to-Westerner relationship. Stick to your guns. At the same time, don't pull them out unless you're ready to shoot.

65. IT'S NOT OVER TIL IT'S OVER

Just in case you forgot about Chapter 45, I'll say it again. In Chinese negotiations, no issues are closed until *all* the issues are closed.   And since all the issues are never really closed, it's never really over.

You won't really know how much you're going to end up paying your painters until they finish and you write the last check... and so on...

66. MY BLACK MONDAY

Monday October 13th, 2003. That was my "last straw" day.

The SARS scare was in the past. I had just come back from my October holiday rock climbing vacation and had to juggle figuring out what to do with the corporate catering business, after Kallie's abrupt departure (Chapter 61), and had to prepare to woo a potential investor who had come to town.

The day started off nicely enough – a warm, sunny and beautifully clear fall day. I had met the potential investor, let's call him "Joe", the day before, so we were past the small talk. The morning was to be spent going over the entire operations. We started at the Central Kitchen, which was the heart and brain of the operations. We housed the office, inventory, kitchen and bakery in about 400 sqm (4000 sqft) in a two-story building. We had a solid operating team, systems for everything and a great production line so the whole tour went very smoothly. We then jumped in a cab to head up to the university café location. That too was a great walk-through. The staff there was the most experienced, everything ran like clockwork and the café didn't require me to be there at all. The third stop was in the little kiosk we had in the lobby at the China Merchant Tower.

As I walked in and before anyone saw me, the kiosk supervisor said my name. I was in a good mood and said, "Hey. You said my name and here I am!" She was not too happy though and she quickly explained to me the real reason Kallie was leaving the company. This was all done in Chinese so the investor didn't understand it at all; but learning that a trusted person was lying, cheating and stealing from you is like being stabbed in the back. As it was a small shop, we only stayed for about five minutes and then walked over to the next shop. I had three locations on the same street about a 15-minute walk from each.

The Silk Alley location was definitely the Crown Jewel in the Beijing Sammies Empire. My heart was with the university location because of the history and the staff, but for sheer visibility, nothing could hold a candle to the Silk Alley spot. We had the corner location facing the busiest street in the city, right beside probably the most popular tourist shopping locations in Beijing. If I was at all shaken by the news from the kiosk supervisor, it was erased when I saw how busy the Silk Alley location was when we walked in. The manager let me know he had a meeting with the landlord later that day at 4:00 and would keep me posted. We didn't stay long because we couldn't get a seat; which was a favorite problem of mine back then.

While walking to the last stop of the tour, I got a call from the landlord of the China Resource kiosk; they wanted to get together later in the week to talk about a "few things." I didn't think too much of it and continued discussing expansion options with Joe, the potential investor. The final location, the Exchange Beijing Tower, was the newest and the most professionally designed. It had all the elements Sammies wanted and needed to roll out more cafés. We had an early lunch, before it got too busy and said goodbye for the day since Joe had some meetings in the afternoon.

On the way back to the office I got a frantic call from the supervisor of the China Resource kiosk. She asked me if there was anything going on with the location. I told her I got a call from the landlord earlier but nothing I knew about; why? She then proceeded to tell me that there was a group of people from Starbucks standing in front of our kiosk, talking and pointing fingers.

Oh...right...

I immediately called the landlord to ask him what was going on. He was a little taken aback but proceeded to tell me that while originally Starbucks did not want to enter the building, which was the reason Sammies got such a sweet deal, they had now decided that they would like to come into the building and he would really appreciate it if we would simply vacate the premises by the end of the month.

The loss of the China Resources kiosk was not such a financial issue because nothing was nailed down, and while profitable, the income was not even a tenth of the university location, but emotionally it hurt. I call that episode getting spit in the face.

So by the time I got to the office, I had two steaming piles of poop to deal with: Kallie and the impending termination of our small kiosk. While working away, I received a call around 4:15 from the Silk Alley manager.

He said I really needed to come down to meet with the landlord. So I jumped into a taxi and 15 minutes later I was walking up to see the Old Horse (Lao Ma).

Mr. Ma looked like he was in his mid-fifties and had the archetypal, China old school, little empire, big boss mannerisms. He dealt with the local mafia, the local government and even young fiery foreigners all with the same calm, unshakable attitude. I liked him and he always treated me well.

So in I walked and he asked me how the weather was. I said it was a beautiful day and he said, "Yes. Remember that and now sit down." He then went on to tell me that he had just had a meeting with this boss and his boss's boss and with his boss's boss's boss. They told him that they had met with the government and that the government would like to cooperate with a real estate developer to develop this land and so they would appreciate if I would leave the location by Friday.

Thud... exhale...

Oh... Right...by Friday. This Friday. Sure. OK...

Before I could even start to make a fuss, I was informed that the water and power was going to be turned off on Friday morning and the demolition would start at 5:00 p.m.

You see in China, the government is Force Majeure and we therefore had zero options. The "deal" we got, was to not have to pay the two months rent that was "waived" during SARS. Apparently, the definition of "waived" was really just meant to be "postponed." Sorry, forgot to send you that message.

I call that episode, "Getting kicked in the crotch."

On the way back to the office I called my Advisory Board, because if I ever needed some advice, now was that day. They told me to look at the numbers and to work out scenarios that would allow Sammies to operate without the two locations and a corporate catering structure that would run on a skeleton crew. Don't forget, this was only months after SARS.

The university location was only operating at 50%, because all the students had been evacuated from the school in the summer and most wouldn't return until the following spring. Sammies was strapped for cash. I stayed in the office till about 10:00 p.m., figuring out a way to keep the company alive.

Almost two years earlier, I had decided it was time for me to get out of the business and allow a professional food and beverage operator run the company. I spent a year upgrading all of our systems and had lined up both a new investor and an Operations Manager before SARS completely derailed all the plans. It was a shame because the March of 2003 was the best month in Sammies history.

Needless to say I was fried. I was already burnt out six months earlier, before SARS. Then with Kallie quitting and taking her customer service girls, well that royally screwed up my little vacation. Finally, to have my hopes of a new investor come in, evaporate in front of me... well, I was completely shattered by the combination: stab in the back, spit in the face and kick in the crotch.

I got home, grabbed the last package of hot chocolate with marshmallows (left by a friend who was my squatter for years), took a quick shower and then sat down with another friend who was squatting at my place to tell him the unbelievable day I just had. I was just finishing the story and about halfway through my hot coco when I noticed I was still chewing on the marshmallows. Thinking that was odd, I spit it out into my hand. I looked at it and then spit out, what I thought was the other marshmallow. It probably took a second before it registered... maggots. There were maggots in my hot chocolate. I believe my response, was, "You have got to be f*@king KIDDING ME!"

I then looked up to the ceiling, hands up in surrender and told God that, "I got it! I'm done. No more, thanks."

The next day I informed my investors that as Sammies' CEO, it was time for the company to get a new President. The current President was completely burnt out, no longer a viable option and would be removed from his post within six months. Since I was the President I knew this was true.

In that meeting with the investors, they could see that the President no longer had the motivation to run the business and should be changed. Two of them did not want me to go and over the next few months, as the company wallowed in the mire, did very little to help with the transition.

Near the end of December, one of the investors who also owned an Italian and an Indian restaurant offered to buy the company. He got it for a song, didn't want my help with any sort of transition and installed his operator to take over the business.

Within 10 months, Beijing Sammies was run into the ground and gone.

Section V

Operations, Finances & Human Resources

THE ALL-YOU-CAN-EAT-BUFFET

Start working on your calming breathing practices now...

67. CHINA'S TALENT PUDDLE

AKA Finding your needle in a hay**field**

Sure with a population of 1.3 BILLION, finding "people" is easy.

The labor force, at the bottom, is made up of around 900 million people. Most are very, very poor and willing to work for next to nothing. So for physical jobs, ones that require very little thought and very little training, you are fine. (That being said, the odds of you needing this level of staff are low. Those kinds of businesses are dominated by local firms that will be able to beat you on price every time.)

BUT, if you are looking for skilled labor, then be prepared to meet with the world's largest talent puddle. It's enormous, mind-bogglingly huge, but very, very shallow.

There's no way a person like you and me can wrap our minds around the number of people competing for even the lowliest of positions. But here's a clue: the same job that would get 50 resumes in the U.S. could easily pull in 500 – 1,000 in China. No joke. Just think of the amount of effort required to wade through all that!

And although 90% of those resumes will be heavily doctored, there is a sizeable talent pool of bright, hard-working, young people ready to fill your lower-level positions.

On the other hand, finding experienced, capable managers is extremely difficult. Why? Almost everyone who applies lacks many of the basic skills and experience any manager needs to be successful. And how could they? This market only opened up in the mid-eighties. There was no past generation of experienced managers to mentor them. (Remember Chapter 13. They're new to this.)

So... how are you going to find quality employees? You will probably do what everyone else does.

As you're just getting started, you will not be in too much of a rush. The first 2-4 weeks will be spent with you asking everyone you know if they know of anyone qualified. If you're not picky, you'll take the first decent person you meet. If you are picky and want to shop around, you will not be happy with the first round. Then in order to get and see "more options," you will place an ad on one of the larger job boards. Then after 2-3 days of getting swamped with fluff, you will begin to get overwhelmed.

Then very shortly afterwards, you will be overwhelmed and every day that goes by you will become more and more frustrated at not being able to find something as simple as an assistant. And this is just the beginning....

68. OUTSOURCE THE TALENT SOURCING

Avoid making this rookie mistake of trying to find talent on your own. Instead of just asking around for someone good, also ask for any recruitment firms people have used and liked. Make sure to ask for the specific person they worked with.

Make finding and sifting through the talent fluff, someone else's priority. The money, stress, time, and confusion this will save you will be worth many times the price you pay. It may be 1-2 months' salary, but don't forget we are talking about a couple hundred dollars a month, NOT a couple thousand.

That being said, having been an executive recruiter in China, what you may learn about the market from the recruiter is worth a great deal of the fee. Make sure to interview the recruiter and look at them like you would look at a consultant or a lawyer. You want a consultant or lawyer you can learn something from. If you can't get this from your recruiter, move on.

If you ARE looking for someone to be on your management team, you better look at the process as one of the most important investments you will make in China. Do NOT see this as a simple HR issue, like you may relegate it in the West. I may have said this already, but *China is not the West.*

You are probably focused on starting your business, but remember, it will be the people you hire who will be getting it done. You will have lots to do. There will be plenty of time spent interviewing, so make sure you spend it interviewing quality people and let someone else do the sorting and sifting for you.

69. ONE CHILD POLICY = LITTLE EMPERORS

In China, between the One Child Policy and the insane pressure placed on kids to study, you get kids that grow up in a warped sense of reality with pretty poor social skills.

Of course, what would you expect when you have 6 people (2 sets of grandparents (4) and the parents (2) all vying for the kids attention? You get a huge number of kids that think they are the center of the universe.

Let's back up a second. In China, Mom and Dad are not like parents in the West. Very often Chinese Moms and Dads don't even raise their child; the grandparents do.

Mom and Dad are out working all day and the kid is left at home to be cared for by the grandparents or even live with the grandparents. I even know of a few parents who only see their two-year-old on weekends.

Now this gets even weirder when you think about the situation when the kid is born and there are 6 people standing around who have NO experience with a newborn. Seriously. My father-in-law, who is a great guy, held a baby for the first time when my daughter Sophie was born. He's got 3 kids!

Generally speaking, grandparents spoil the kid. They want the kid to like them, to have fun during the time they spend with them.

What are the chances you'd develop a massive sense of entitlement? Pretty good, huh?

That's why plenty of your young Chinese employees are going to be even more arrogant, and carry around an even bigger sense of entitlement, than your average Western teenager or twenty-something.

Add to that the fact that they were studying, studying, studying math, practicing the piano, studying English, or preparing for a test while their Western counterparts were playing together, spending time with their boyfriend or girlfriend, or working a part-time job and you can understand why their social skills usually leave a lot to be desired.

Then don't forget that with the whole face thing, all the family's hopes and expectations being focused on the only child is like a magnifying glass in the sun, all beating down on junior's head.

70. EDUCATION INSANITY

Before we go on with HR, let's take a small step back and take a look at the system that created your employees – the education system.

As we have already pointed out, with so many people, China operates within a "Jungle" mentality; competition is fierce! What this translates into is incredible pressure on a child to perform well in school. If a child doesn't score well in elementary school, they won't get into a "good" middle school and if they don't score well in middle school, they won't get into a "good" high school. And a child who hasn't attended a "good" high school can forget about college. Every year before the university exam, thousands of parents flock to the various temples to PRAY for their kid to do well on the upcoming exam.

A "college-free" life isn't a life in which a budding young entrepreneur gets an early start in the business world or a talented carpenter is busy making a name for himself in his community before he even hits 20.

No, it's a life spent at a depressing factory job, menial labor or worse. It's a life spent dealing with pissed off parents and grandparents. Very, very pissed-off parents and grandparents. Parents and grandparents who have lost face because of you and aren't going to let you forget it, mister.

Chinese children are already under incredible pressure to perform academically. So while their American counterparts are blissfully scrunching Play Doh into various pretend creatures, water-painting and playing dress-up, their parents are breathing down their necks to protect their family's face (or add to it!).

Even China's most imaginative children must first quash their talents and become championship memorizers and fact regurgitators. So it's no wonder by the time they reach university, that their willingness to share their creative ideas when they have them, is almost non-existent.

71.   FACE & THE CREATIVITY CRISIS

You need to be crystal clear that thinking "inside the box" has a long tradition in China. It's a cultural habit. And it's a hard habit to break – especially when just about everyone in the society "thinks" it's how things should be done.

Sure, the education system and decades of state suppression and anti-intellectualism have made keeping your head down and your mouth shut the safest route for just about everyone. But China's creativity crisis really started with Confucianism's emphasis on hierarchy. Remember, they can't lose face by doing things the way they've always been done. That's thousands of years of anti-creativity at work in the culture – and in a realllly big way.

As we have said, the Chinese school system pretty much rewards conformity and stifles creativity, and that has a lasting impact on each and every student educated there. Teachers and learning programs focus on memorization and rote learning, rather than on problem-solving skills and what we like to call "out-of-the-box" thinking, or innovation. And the nation's testing protocols are set up to reflect this paradigm. When you're tested and rewarded based on your ability to conform, you're likely to become very good at conforming and NOT thinking outside the box.

So, what does this mean for you, as an employer?

The bright ideas, new ways of looking at things and flexibility that young people bring into Western organizations are likely to be non-existent. You can't count on the natural brainstorming Western employees do together when faced with a problem that arises while you're off site.

For the most part, you're probably going to have to be the team problem-solver, the risk-taker and the "out of the box" thinker.

Of course, you can do yourself (and the future of your employees) a great service by making creative exercises a part of your team's working life, by encouraging your employees to take risks. You can emphasize that the only stupid ideas are the ones no one shoots at you when you're looking for an answer. You can let your people know, again and again, that being willing to take creative risks is something you admire and will reward with praise and promotions.

If you want to receive input from your contractors or employees, ask for it. Ask for it again and again, until a few hardy souls give it a shot – and don't get shot, themselves. Then, when you get it, reward those who took a chance on you and spoke up.

But what you will probably find is....

72.   LET'S PLAY FOLLOW THE BOSS

Thanks to their rigid social training and conformity-rewarding educational experiences, your employees are almost always going to have an infuriating tendency to do exactly what you tell them to do – no more and no less. (Or, at least, what they *think* you're telling them to do!)

If you're a micro manager and enjoy systematizing each and every task you want your employees to carry out, you'll be in heaven. But if you want to give a project to an on-the-ball employee and let them run with it, you'd better be sure they're ready.   Most of the time, you'll save yourself a multitude of headaches by supervising your team members much more closely than you'd even think about supervising them at home in the West. You'll want to give them simple, clear, complete instructions – and perhaps even assign them one step at a time.

Unlike some employees in the West, most Mainland China employees may actually appreciate the fact that at the beginning, you're coaching them, practically looking over their shoulder while they work. It will make them feel safe, secure and on target. Then once they are cool with what needs to be done, you can move on and they can feel "free" to do what they need to do.

You can also expect that most of the time your employees will do what you and/or anyone higher up in the hierarchy tell them to do without offering suggestions or giving input about what they see as potential pitfalls.

It's not that they don't care about you or the company. It's that their culture teaches that questioning authority is disrespectful – a "face" faux pas at best and an unforgivable insult, at worst. And don't forget, by suggesting something, they run the risk of being wrong, which would lose them face.

Taking any sort of risk, such as stepping off the clearly demarcated yellow brick road, rarely happens, which tends to make a "team effort" difficult.

73. IF YOU NEED ONE PERSON, CHOOSE THE CHINESE; IF YOU NEED A TEAM, DON'T CHOOSE THE CHINESE.

In Mainland China, the "teamwork!" model prized in the West is virtually non-existent. Employees here want to know EXACTLY what they are responsible for, and therefore, clear about exactly what they are NOT responsible for. Having such black and white boundaries are difficult to define when dealing with a team.

Let me spell it out for you: Chinese do not work so well together in a team (unless the team is more like an assembly line with each person having their tasks clearly separated and defined).

This may be a combination of a number of factors (Little Emperor Syndrome, lack of creativity, face saving techniques, the need to know who can boss who around, etc) but for you... you need to be crystal clear about this. Do **not** expect your proven Western management style to just seamlessly work here.

Remember, they may have very little experience working as a team or in a team, so expect to spend a lot more time writing rules, procedures, and policies. Then expect to invest a great deal of time coaching your team how to act like a team. One weekend at a team building retreat is a good start, but it's just a start.

74. THE POWER OF SYSTEMATIZED SUCCESS

If you want your people to work hard for you, create a system that responsibly and reliably rewards hard work. Come up with objectives that can be clearly and reliably measured, so there's no doubt in your mind or theirs when your employees meet them.

This is good business practice in the West, but it's even more important in mainland China, because you should not expect your employees to be plagued with guilt when and if they under-perform. There is no cultural buy-in to the philosophy that hard work is its own reward and naturally leads to financial success. This means that many of our employees are NOT intrinsically motivated to consistently perform at a high level.

In China, extrinsic, transparent, performance-based rewards are highly important to employees – just about everyone is driven by not losing face and then by financial rewards... which once gained are a source of, yes, you guessed it, face.

Your employees and team members need to be able to see **exactly** what they need to do to *work the system*, in their favor. You must have a system that ties individual goals with the goals of the company.

System dictates behavior, yo.

If they don't see it, expect that many of them (especially those with whom you have not had time and/or opportunity to build a strong relationship) will work the system in their favor.

For some, they feel as if they are entitled to it.

75. YOU MUST BE THE ALPHA DOG

Keep the lines of authority clear.

Your employees need this to feel you can be trusted, that their jobs are secure and that you'll maintain order among everyone – because they've been taught to find safety in hierarchy.

Sammies Moment
When we opened our corporate catering business, we were happy to discover that most of our new delivery guys were great kids, hard workers. But one guy was more than a little rough around the edges, and he gave one of our customers attitude. So the catering manager decided he had to go.

Well, she fired him and told him exactly why. (Big mistake! Not the firing, but the honesty.)

He became angry and agitated and started yelling at her, calling her names. I was in the next office when it started happening, and I heard the volume increase through the wall. Since the manager was about 100 pounds soaking wet, it took me about a second and a half to get in there and say "This conversation is over."

A second later, we were in a pushing match, which lasted until he ran into the kitchen, grabbed a knife and started to come after me. With the adrenalin rushing, I was like "Bring it on! Let's do it!" In the blink of an eye, the guys in the kitchen rushed around him, held him back, took the knife from his hand and led him out the door.

The next day, he came back acting like it had never happened. "Oh, Sam, you know I wasn't going to hurt you! I would never do that!" No apologies. (Not that it would have mattered.) This is par for the course in a land where almost no one cops to their mistakes – even when they're glaringly obvious.

But the real point of this story is this: I got tons of face for being the tough guy. My employees loved it, loved that they could be proud of their boss. They went home and told their friends and family that I was "the man."

You certainly do NOT need a knife fight to show you are the boss, but you can forget being a buddy. To be the boss, you have to BE THE BOSS.

76. EMOTIONAL EXTREMES

In China, small businesses are intensely personal. Your China team will become like family to you. Here, your employees are either all in, or just putting in the time until something better comes by.

Loyalty here is an honored virtue. It's a value held very close to the hearts of your Chinese employees. If you're loyal to them and make sure they know it, they'll be loyal to you and your company in a way rarely found in America, Canada or anywhere else in the West.

When we had to move all the equipment out of Sammies in the middle of the night to save the business from my cheating partner, my team members pitched in and worked their butts off to get the job done in time. No complaints. No bitching or moaning. We were a team.

Some of my Beijing Sammies' staff members were so loyal that if someone made a disparaging comment about Sammies, they were ready to go to fisticuffs.

I have literally had to tell employees to go home when they were tired from pushing so hard to make the business a success. The only way to get them out the door to take care of themselves was to tie it to their sense of responsibility to all of us in the store: "If you get sick, you won't be able to help us next week during the rush."

With this kind of loyalty comes responsibility. A responsibility to recognize and reward your employees for going the extra mile – which they will do.

A responsibility to refrain from taking advantage of their affection for you.

A responsibility to treat them with respect and honor in a very Chinese way:

- Always being mindful of saving and giving them face
- Moderating your emotional reactions
- Watching your tone of voice when you correct their work (because they will multiply your stated displeasure by at least ten)

77. IT'S NEVER THEIR FAULT

Growing up, I used to love those kung-fu movies when the hero would, with some super cool lightning fast moves, deflect the 1000 arrows fired at him. That was cool stuff. However, when my staff would use the verbal equivalent to deflect any and all responsibility from mistakes made, I never thought that was remotely cool.

What happens when parents, the government, teachers, and just about every other social structure punish mistakes harshly? When one small screw-up could result in a loss of face for not just you, but for your company or entire family as well?!

You get a bunch of people who can't afford (psychologically or practically) to be wrong and you get a bunch of people who refuse to take responsibility for their mistakes – at least in words and in public.

In the West, making mistakes (at least while you're trying to do something new or innovative) is tolerated. Often, a willingness to make mistakes in the pursuit of a goal is even encouraged by smart employers who want to make the most of their employees' talents and initiative. People who always feel they have to play it safe don't accomplish much, after all.

When you're tempted to get pissed off at an employee's refusal to take responsibility for their own actions, imagine what it would be like to live with the threat of career annihilation and social alienation hanging over your head. Because that's what working life feels like to your employees. Like a cartoon anvil hanging over their head at all times – only it's not funny at all.

They haven't been taught "if at first you don't succeed, try, try again!" Instead, they've been taught that making a mistake causes you to lose face, and losing face exacts a high price – not just in personal terms, but in career and financial terms, as well. Every employee knows there are at least fifty people lined up behind them, ready to take their job – five or ten times as many people as there would be in the U.S., at least.

So, how can you deal with this?

First, make sure clear lines of accountability are drawn and you have the system in place so success or failure-to-perform can be directly tied to compensation. Ming Lee is responsible for taking inventory every week. Pang Hua is in charge of the team's schedule. Esther Wang is responsible for keeping the marketing materials up to date and in stock.

Second, when you assign specific tasks to specific people, put the assignments in writing and have them sign it. This helps your employee stay straight about what's expected, so they'll know they really can't sidestep responsibility. (Just make sure you have a copy so you can pull it out if you need to, in order to get to the heart of the matter if something goes awry.)

Third, show your employees exactly how you want things done, whenever possible.

Fourth, make sure your employees have the knowledge, skills, tools and supplies they need in order to succeed.

Fifth, demonstrate to your employees through your words and actions that you will respond fairly when they screw up - as long as they take responsibility!

Let them know that the worst mistake they can make is passing the buck.

If you fail to do the above, you will surely face the nothing-sticks-to-me tai-chi, kung-fu combination that results in money flowing like water out of your company.

Meditate on that grasshopper...

78. PRAISE QUIETLY

I was taught to punish in private and praise in public. Other than the wonderful Chinese idiom "Kill the chicken and let the monkey see," where you make an example out of someone small so the bigger problem gets in line, I would say to keep it all private.

Because Guanxi is such a factor, if you praise a worker in public, you run the risk of having them and others think they are now the "Golden Child". If this happens and you then need to correct the person, they can lose tremendous face and you may end up losing a star (albeit emotionally fragile) employee.

When do you pass out the kudos, curb your enthusiasm. Let them know you are happy with them, but don't let them think they are indispensable. Praise their efforts not their talent.

Just be prepared, regardless of what you do, you will eventually have to make some changes and maybe even let some people go.

79. THE "G" WORD

The basics:

1) China is not a God-Fearing country.
2) The Chinese are probably the most pragmatic people you'll ever meet.

I'll just come right out and say it, a large percentage of the Chinese who "find God", do so for practical purposes; for Guanxi. The later they find God, the more cynical my view.

Overall, God is not a *given* in China. He/She has some fans, even some groupies and it's not like (S)He's "unpopular," in China, but (S)He's certainly not a smart conversational choice. In general, a person's religious preferences are best considered private.

80. THE DARK SIDE OF FACE & CREATIVITY

Shhh... come closer. I don't want to say this too loudly here....

Everything I just said in the past few chapters is true but not always...

In fact, you may find the Chinese exceptionally creative...when it comes to manipulative or shady tactics. You may come to believe that the average Chinese are at heart lawyers, because of their seemingly innate ability to creatively define or re-work the system to their benefit.

I'm not saying they are there to screw you over; I am saying they will try, and will find a way to "game" your system in a way that benefits them.

And if they can find a way, remember it's because they were clever enough and you were dumb enough to let it happen. (Remember about getting conned?) And don't think they are going to lose any sleep over it, as if gaming *your* system is going to lose *them* face.

No...They are won't see this as making a mistake, nor will they see this as breaking any rules. They are just being clever.

I know what you are thinking... *If only they could use their creative powers for GOOD!*

But wait, there's more...

81. "IT'S WRONG TO STEAL... A LOT"

In China, there seems to be a cultural acceptance of petty thievery. This doesn't apply so much to friends and family members, but it certainly applies to bosses and businesses.

Once, at Beijing Sammies we were preparing to cater a business lunch for hundreds of people who worked for a Fortune 500 company. It was their "outdoors" day and they wanted to brown bag the lunch so they could grab n' go.

I wanted to set all the food up like an assembly line: sandwiches, sides, fruit, desserts, and so on, instead of packing the lunches individually in brown bags. It was easier for us to transport, faster to people to get the combination they wanted and people wouldn't end up with smashed sandwiches and crushed cookies, etc.

The sales woman who'd gotten us the job was a very sweet, proper young lady, almost naïve. In the U.S., you'd call her a "librarian" type.

"No, Sam, we can't do it that way," she told me. "People will steal. They won't steal whole lunch bags, but if we spread everything out, and they go through a line, they'll take an extra snack or a dessert. Before we get through everyone, we'll have run out."

She went on to explain that in China, the overwhelming majority of people would consider taking an entire lunch bag wrong, but just about everyone feels okay about taking a little bit extra of this or that.

I called a Chinese friend and asked, "Could this be true?" He assured me it most certainly was true and then he asked me how I'd made it in China as long as I had, given I was such a dumbass.

It comes down to this: such a little amount, of anything, would mean so *little* to the company, but to them, it would mean a *lot*.

Be aware, there are a lot of people who think like this, customers and employees alike. So, a little bit here, a little bit there… add it up and you are out of business my friend. Set up service practices and protocols that make petty thievery close to impossible – or pay the price.

At Sammies for instance, we did two things. One, we tied bonuses to sales and cost-of-goods expenses. Since even a small swipe raises the cost of goods, employees will naturally be on the look-out for those whose sticky fingers might mess it up for everyone else. And two, we had a sign at the cash register, "If you don't get a receipt, the food is free," thereby making the customers the police against sticky fingers at the cash register.

JR PURCHASER HAS A BMW

dirty little marketing secret

Quite often, sales people earn based on commissions. So what happens when they can't seem to win by playing by all the rules? Creativity kicks in and this creates kickbacks, AKA the very common "personal incentive bonus plan."

Some background first…

As we all know, in many companies there are "gatekeepers" and "key masters." The Purchaser is in a very crappy position. Even if they are totally clean, everyone thinks that they're on the take. They are constantly given "incentives" from suppliers to choose their product over others.

It works like this…

- The manager gets the information about the 10% discount and thinks they are doing well, when actually it's a 15% discount.
- The Company gets the official receipts for the 10% and then the supplier gives the Purchaser an additional 5% "off the books" rebate.

In their minds, it's not that they are stealing from the company (wait, this is an interesting way of looking at things) because the company would not have gotten the 15% rebate but only the 10% rebate. Or so the story goes.

But it goes deeper than this. Secretaries and HR managers get to play too. Who does the ordering for travel tickets, food, or outings? Who makes the final call for housing suppliers, medical insurance, etc?

Don't think of the individual transactions, because these are nominal, but when they are multiplied over multiple people and many months, it probably adds up to a pretty hefty increase from the meager salary that person is probably getting.

Just ask yourself the question, "What's in it for me?" for every person your company comes into contact with.

Sammies Moment
At Sammies, our corporate accounts received 'points' for every order they made online. There were a number of opportunistic secretaries who would pool orders for the office and on weekends have deliveries made to their homes, or simply receive a 20% discount, pocketing the difference. Did the people ordering ever ask? Probably not.

Did we plan for this? No, but my customer service manager knew this would happen (and probably added a few more corporate clients to the list by informing the gatekeepers of this nifty trick.)

83.   HONESTY &
THE THIRD ACCOUNTING BOOK

"Honest" in China has two meanings.
1. The traditional meaning, the one you are thinking.
2. The meaning people use when talking about some naïve, foolish, green sap that does everything according to the letter of the law.

So look out when your partner describes you as "honest" to another local.

I'm sure you are aware of unscrupulous companies that keep two sets of accounting books: one for the tax man and one with the real numbers. Well in China, be aware that some companies have taken this to the next level: introducing the third accounting book – the one for the investors.

China Moment
At the early stage of my latest company, an IT, Web 2.0, EBay for hired services called Me-2-B.com, I hired a project manager to be the interface between me and the developers. I'm not from the industry so Anthony took care of finding and hiring the developers. Since we were a small operation and just getting started, I was lax in my management and left Anthony responsible for the few general administrative tasks. Anthony found the staff, hired them and paid them every month. For those of you

who are experienced, you probably already see the problem. For those who are inexperienced and believe trust is a fundamental premise in any relationship, hold on.

The practice of having a third book for investors is so pervasive, that when Anthony hired a few of the developers he told them they would get paid X amount, but the amount in their contract would be X+Y amount. "That's the amount we tell the investors", he would casually say, and no one thought any different. I only found out during the month that Anthony was a little too late with salaries and a new guy asked me when he would receive his 2,400rmb; in Anthony's monthly expense report it said 4,200rmb.

I made a cardinal mistake leaving too much power in the hands of one person, but the crazy thing was that no one ever said anything about the discrepancy in received and reported salaries. They all thought it was normal. Fact was, Anthony was pocketing the difference.

When we did call the police, they said it was a matter for the courts and Anthony did a runner. No one has seen or heard from him since. If you ever do see him, let me know, I know a guy who knows a guy who would like to have "a few words" with him.

84. IN LIFE, YOU CHOOSE YOUR OWN BATTLES

If you get screwed by a Chinese partner, supplier or customer, think long and hard before investing the time and money that a legal battle will cost you. If you get sued, strongly consider paying up.

Yes, the Chinese legal system is notorious for favoring Chinese companies and concerns over foreign interests.

It's even better known for favoring workers' causes over the rights of Chinese businesses, giving the benefit of the doubt to the worker(s) in question and the evil eye to the greedy, money-hungry corporation. If you're a foreigner or a mainland corporation and you have tons of evidence and/or witnesses lined up to vouch for you against a "simple worker," you might come out ahead. Otherwise, odds are good that all you'll have to show for your efforts will be attorney bills.

Here, the rule of law could go like this: "You are innocent until proven wealthier than your accuser."

I know of many cases in which a mainland Chinese business has settled an obviously fraudulent claim by a "little guy" just to avoid battling the communist mindset that still prevails in the Chinese judicial system. In the

Chinese courts, socialist principles have more power than any legal statute or precedent.

Once, I had to defend myself against a completely unfounded wrongful dismissal claim. I had, in my hands, proof that the other side falsified documents and changed their story. I was told to pay up anyway, because the amount my (false) accuser demanded would mean "so little" to me and "so much" to him!

I could blame it on being a foreigner, but the same thing happens to Mainland Chinese companies all the time.

My advice: if you are wronged or sued, hire someone to suffer through your legal headaches in your place and wash your hands of it the best you can. Better yet, brush it off completely and focus your energies on making your business better.

85. DON'T FIRE THEM... TRANSFER THEM!

When it comes to employer-employee disputes, the employee is pretty much always right – at least in the eyes of the courts.

You must remember that China's judges, mediators and arbitrators came of age in a society where capitalism was, by definition, evil. It could not exist without exploiting workers, or so they were taught. So, there's a natural tendency to rule in the worker's favor when they accuse a company (especially a foreign company!) of any kind of wrongdoing.

If it's not that mindset, you have either the old school "Iron Rice Bowl" mentality that it's the State's job to provide for workers, or the new school "it-will-mean-so-little-to-you-but-so-much-to-them." Then don't forget the pervading belief that foreign companies are rich and can certainly afford to foot the bill. If you get sued, you will probably lose.

So, don't get sued. Don't take risks with labor laws.

If you can, first sign a three month contract. If that doesn't work (and it probably won't with really talented people), use the probation period to really test the worker. Keeping the contract period to a reasonable length gives the employer the option to continue or not.

Letting someone go in the middle of their contract is often expensive. Let me tell you how most Chinese deal with it. Remember how nothing is done in a straight line?

Remember how the ends do justify the means? Well, when firing someone costs a lot of money and it's a small company... people tend to get transferred. (I don't think this is a new idea, nor do I think the Chinese invented it, but it's very common.)

Move their job to another city where they're not even going to think about moving, demote them to work they'll never tolerate, or send them to the branch where their over-achieving cousin that they hate is running the show.

Do whatever you have to do to get them out of your hair without actually giving them the ax.

I was sued for wrongful dismissal after I fired a low-level employee for doing a bad job and breaking the rules. I lost, even though the employee was caught lying on the record and falsifying evidence.

The arbitrator asked me why I would waste my time dealing with such a small-potato issue, instead of just paying up and running my business. I wasn't about to do that, because I knew that if I took it for this kid, I'd be taking it for a long line of similar young pains in the behind, all wanting a piece of the action.

Surprise, surprise! That's exactly what happened. Don't forget I had a rough bunch working for me; delivery boys and kitchen staff are not college graduates.

Suing foreign companies has become another way for the dregs of Chinese society to make money. The disgusting thing is, the companies that are really horrible to their employees, genuinely exploiting and mistreating their workers, have the connections to stay above the fray. They go on doing business as usual, while mom-and-pop shops and decent companies get raked over the coals again and again.

I should say something about not dating your employees, but I didn't follow this one, myself. But I married her, so it worked out.

Section VI

Dealing with the Government

Just imagine something witty about lying down with snakes or swimming with sharks or rolling around in manure... the odds are you are not going to come out of the experience unscathed.

86. GIVE SMALL-TIME OFFICIALS BIG-TIME FACE

He's a representative from the sanitation bureau, a health inspector, a licensing dictator. He's got a *small* office, a *small* salary, a *small* apartment, and disappointed parents. He wants you to give him *big face*.

At a minimum, always, always, always be polite. If you fail to give small-time officials face, you can expect trouble. Not always from their department. (That would be too straightforward.) But a cool comment or thoughtless oversight may give new purpose to someone who'll turn out to be a "mailroom dictator," and is sure to have "friends" in other departments.

Don't say...

"But you said the files were fine!"

"But the guy who was here the other day took a check with him!"

"We can't get any work done because you guys are always here, up our butts."

"Is this really going to be it? Will we really be done now?"

Do say...

"I'm so glad you pointed that out. We had no idea!"

"Wow! We tried to turn in all the forms. I guess we missed one!"

"We really appreciate how patient you've been with us, through this process."

Let me put it this way. When a bureaucratic reviews your paperwork or shows up at your site, they are there to find something wrong. And you can bet they will. But don't sweat it. That's why you've got Guanxi or "Guanxi-for-hire" in your back pocket.

Now, let's get real. If running into difficulties with government officials on a regular basis is going to stress you out, you'd better find a line of work other than starting or building a business in China.

All that being said, you can minimize the "irregularities", "oversights" and "violations" they find when they're going through your stuff with a fine tooth comb by giving them lots and lots and lots of face.

I'm not talking about cowing or meowing, you should have someone to do that for you. And don't roll over and do everything a small-time official tells you to do, you'll advertise yourself as a "push-over." Before you know it, a line will form outside your door made up of fellow bureaucrats who want their slice of the rich foreigner's pie. And the farther you are from the first-tier cities, the more this principle holds.

But if you can hold back a little, while giving big-time face, you'll avoid a lot of heartache, and maybe even make a new "friend," er, I mean some guanxi.

87. HIRE A HANDLER, ALREADY

You need to have someone on your team or on call who can handle your personal government bureaucrats. I'm talking about those officials who will be in your business. Literally. In. Your. Business. Way too much of the time!

There's no way a Westerner like you or me will ever truly "get it," ever be able to negotiate the ins and outs of Chinese bureaucracy. To even develop a modicum of "handling" skills you'd have to devote such a significant percentage of your time, you could not possibly run your business!

Your handler should...

- o Have experience dealing with bureaucrats – possibly from the "inside."
- o Have real, substantial "Guanxi" at their disposal.
- o Be a team player – and ready to make spontaneous decisions within pre-set limits.

I had a great handler for years. She was in her fifties, an old school government employee who decided to use her Guanxi in the private sector. In the winter, she would wear seven-eight layers of clothing and looked like a butterball turkey. All she did was deal with government officials who came by, take them out to dinner, buy them cigarettes, and drop in on the bureaus every month with goodies and gossip for everyone in the office. (The best defense is a good offense!)

She was worth every dollar I paid her – and many more. So when the new people came to take over the business, they got rid of her and within ten months the company was out of business, due to a "broken rule."

I am over simplifying the situation, because they made a number of bad moves, and this "last straw" really just gave them the opportunity to blame someone else.

More importantly for what you're learning here: the situation probably never would have happened if my handler had been on the job.

All in all, unless you are fluent in Chinese (not just the language, but the culture) and love swimming in shark-infested waters, pay someone else to deal with that crap. Trust me, you'll have plenty of other crap to deal with, my friend.

88. GIVING GOOD FACE

What are you going to do when you are cornered by one of the small-time government types?

These are the 3 F's of giving face.

1. Flattery
2. Favors
3. Fancy gifts

Remember them, and you'll do fine.

Let's start with flattery. You probably cannot say enough nice things to one of these guys. I suck at this, but my butterball handler was awesome at it. She would throw out compliments that would be viewed as embarrassingly over the top and they seemed just about right:

"You are the smartest, savviest, most gifted accountant I have ever known!"

"I could never have imagined I would be so fortunate as to have the opportunity to lunch with someone of your accomplishments and taste."

Honestly, I don't know how she did it with a straight face.

Now, let's talk about favors. Favors aren't always done to help out immediately, they are seen as investments.

You need to get an operating license for your new manufacturing arm. You know someone who knows someone who knows someone who might be able to help you get one in three months as opposed to six. While pulling this string you can expect to get a call in the future from someone who you will be expected to help out. Quid pro quo...

And don't forget to give *fancy gifts*. Giving someone face by giving them gifts is an integral part of the business relationship-building process in China. It's important that you give people you want to impress or please, gifts they can show off. There's no value in a mediocre, quaint, charming or folksy gift unless it's truly unique, and those gifts are better for your partner than for one-off transactional-government-official-types. (A shiny piece of your country's currency, like an American silver dollar, is not a gift; it's a *joke* - unless it's for the kid or parent of your partner who you know collects currencies.) Of course it depends on the recipient, but if you are dealing with small time officials make sure the packaging is flashy and expensive-looking. As a matter of fact, in China, it's not unusual for a gift's wrapping to cost more than the gift itself.

A quick note about when you want to take potential partners and prospects out to dinner. That charming "hole-in-the-wall" café or mom and pop ethnic eatery that might knock the socks off a client in the West will not impress a Chinese client. If they have never eaten that cuisine before it might even embarrass them. You want to go safe and pricey, choosing a place that's been vetted by knowledgeable Chinese friends or colleagues; most likely an expensive, exclusive restaurant. (In China, some restaurants are actually known for their "face value.")

REPEAT AFTER ME: "I CAN'T FOLLOW ALL THE RULES."

The Chinese bureaucracy is complex and convoluted, and the rules change all the time – seemingly every day!

If you try to follow every single rule, you will find it impossible to do business, because nobody can ever determine what the rules are, much less decide how to actually follow them with any accuracy. And that includes the government. (I'm pretty sure they did this on purpose. It means that bureaucratic officials have a lot of latitude to walk into your business at any moment and say "Gotcha!")

Before you freak out, throw your arms up in despair or give up before you even get started, remember the two most important Rules of doing business in China:

Rule #1: There's always a way.
Rule #2: There's always a better way.

Quick anecdote

A few years ago, you didn't need a special license to drive a scooter in Beijing. So, when my buddy got ready to split the mainland and offered to sell me his Vespa-clone scooter for 800rmb (the equivalent of about $100 USD), I said "Sure!"

I probably saved myself the 800rmb in taxi fares in the first two months, and spent two years zipping around the city, having a blast. (Don't worry, Mom! I wore my helmet.)

At some point the law changed, and a scooter license became a "requirement." A license was pricey – more than the cost of the scooter. But the cops didn't really enforce the law, so there were a bunch of unlicensed foreigners (of whom I was one), out on their bikes every day, taking their chances.

The first time I got stopped, I suddenly couldn't seem to remember any Chinese. So, after I spent three minutes smiling and looking confused, the cop just waved me along. Six months later, I got pulled over again. This time I spoke Chinese, told the truth (that I'd bought it from a friend and had just never gotten a license) and got waved along again. The third time was the charm, when the police were cracking down in preparation for the 2008 Olympics. Sigh... I miss my bike.

A good buddy of mine has a very different story. In fact, his is one of the only stories I've ever heard where someone actually followed a surprisingly clear rule and was able to thumb his nose (in his mind) at a cop.

My buddy spent thousands of dollars and had someone on his staff spend a lot of time slicing their way through red tape to get his license, so when he was pulled over, he found himself in a plum position.

"What's the problem, officer?"

"No license."

"Oh, but I do have a license!"

The cop absent-mindedly continued writing his ticket, saying he didn't have to look, because he knew the guy couldn't be properly licensed. In Beijing there are different licenses that dictate how far into the city center you can go.

"I really do have a license! Look!"

Finally, the cop looked and was at a loss for words.

"Thanks, officer! I will be sure to be careful. You have a nice day!"

I know that for my buddy, the pleasure of that moment made the money and time he invested in actually following one of the few straightforward (though rarely enforced) rules on the books in China more than worth it.

What makes this story particularly interesting and entertaining is the fact that clearly being on the right side of the law is such a rare occurrence in China it's worthy of… a story!

89. NEVER PICK FIGHTS WITH 800-LB GORILLAS

When I was a kid, my oldest sister used to love to play that game where she would grab my arm and smack me with it all the while saying, "Why are you hitting yourself? Why are you hitting yourself?"

Who knew that there was a valuable business lesson to be learned in that?

Well, here in China, as a small business, trying to take on the government is basically the same thing.

Repeat after me: The government is always right... The government is always right... The government is always right... The government is always right...

The Chinese government is made up of a lot of octogenarians who are trying their hardest to hold on to a system that has less and less connection with the people – and with the way life is really being lived in China right now.

They don't want to relinquish their power.

Basically, the government and the Chinese people have a deal: "You don't bitch or balk, and we'll leave you alone." What they're saying is that they want lip service and don't rock the boat.

Give it to them. Don't bitch about the rules. Don't moan about the regulations.

Just take a cue from the Buddha and become like water, flowing in, around and through all the obstacles the government sets up for you.

Here are a few examples of phrases that should never pass your lips when in front of a government official

- o "What the hell are you thinking?"
- o "What the hell are they thinking?"
- o "That makes absolutely no sense at all!"
- o "That's not fair!"
- o "Americans would never put up with that."
- o "The way we do it in Canada is so much better."
- o "The system is messed up."

Don't try to argue them into seeing the light. You won't win. To bend to your ideas would mean losing face. And that's just not an option for them. So save yourself the stress and publicly kiss up to them like everyone else – or at least keep your trap shut.

Remember you are in their sandbox.

They are thinking, "Hey! If you don't like it here, go home." And you know – they're right.

90. DANGER! DANGER! WILL ROBINSON!

AKA The Government is not a good business partner

You are in their sandbox.

They pretty much hold all the cards.

Forget contracts.

They ARE the Guanxi.

Legal repercussions… not something they have to worry so much about.

Hmmmm… Sounds like a bad business partner.

OK.

OK.

I'm assuming you are not hugely loaded down with bags of money or come from royalty.

So if you are a small time operator and you are trying to make a deal with the government, I feel for you. Maybe, maybe, if you are thinking "Short term" play (more like one night stand), low expectations…. then you may have a good time.

Not a long lasting relationship.

In fact, I bet the whole affair will end up more like a story to tell the boys after a few drinks than something you will take home to show the folks.

Section VII

Mega Markets

Holy crap Batman!
Look at all those people!

91.   AVOID THE FIRST-TIER CITIES

First-tier cities are easier and more comfortable for foreigners to live in, which means we gravitate to them – whether we're setting up new corporate offices, proven franchises, or new mom-and-pop shops.

Just about every foreign entrepreneur sees the massive money percolating into Beijing, Shanghai, Shenzhen and Guangzhou and heads straight for it, only to discover that large corporations are already dominating their market. Don't be one of them.

Those markets that seem to be wide-open in those giant metropolitan areas are probably that way for good reason. Either people with ideas like yours have already come and gone, wiped out by the city's refusal to buy like Westerners, or they're in the process of being divvied up by conglomerates.

My friend, why make it hard on yourself? Avoid the rush and get where the getting's good – or at least better. Go second or third-tier.

Many markets that are saturated in Beijing and Shanghai are (genuinely) wide-open in over-looked, but rapidly developing second-tier cities like Tianjin, Wuhan and Nanjing. Labor costs are about a quarter of what they are in first-tier cities. The cities are literally "under construction," with infrastructure being built now that will support massive commerce in the future. And best of all, the government bureaucracies are generally a lot less intrusive.

Now, I do have to warn you that some corporations are setting their sights on these hidden opportunities, so the landscape may change quickly. But they're still a much better bet than the four "biggies."

So, get a glass of iced tea or a cold beer, tote this book over to your computer, and spend some time exploring these second-tier cities online. You may just be blown away by the possibilities.

In the North East...
o Dalian
o Shenyang
o Tianjin
o Harbin

In the West...
o Wuhan
o Chongqing
o Chengdu

On the West Coast...

- Nanjing
- Hangzhou
- Suzhou
- Ningbo

Don't forget all the cities in China with over a million people in them. The possibilities truly are enormous.

92. THE NOUVEAU RICHE NICHE

I'll say it again. Luxury means face. Chinese want face. Sell face.

Find a second-, third- or fourth-tier city, one of the hundreds over-a-million-strong, find the most prominent location and plant your flag: "You can't afford this." Staff it with beautiful people with attitude and watch the magic happen.

You may see some of these cities as being far, far behind Beijing and Shanghai, but THAT is why the residents will climb over each other to get what you have.

As an example, there are real estate developers that go from one to the next "over-a-million-strong, country-bumpkin, fourth-tier" cities and put up luxury compounds; twenty units, over a million bucks a pop. All they need is one location in each city and they are laughing, all...the...way...to... the... bank. But be warned: the retail business in China is tough.

- o Finding good locations is not easy.
- o Getting good locations is even tougher and don't expect them to be cheap.
- o Competition is growing -There are a number of players targeting the top 5% of the population (that's why I said to go beyond the first-tier cities)

93. FACE & THE BEAUTY BIZ

Do I really have to say anything about this?

Isn't it obvious by now?

This **is** China's fastest growing industry.

Face. Face. Face. Face. Face. Face. Face. Face. Face. Face.
Image. Image. Image. Image. Image. Image. Image.
Face. Face. Face. Face. Face. Face. Face. Face. Face. Face.
Image. Image. Image. Image. Image. Image. Image.
Face. Face. Face. Face. Face. Face. Face. Face. Face. Face.
Image. Image. Image. Image. Image. Image. Image.
Face. Face. Face. Face. Face. Face. Face. Face. Face. Face.
Image. Image. Image. Image. Image. Image. Image.
Face. Face. Face. Face. Face. Face. Face. Face. Face. Face.
Image. Image. Image. Image. Image. Image. Image.
Face. Face. Face. Face. Face. Face. Face. Face. Face. Face.
Image. Image. Image. Image. Image. Image. Image.
Face. Face. Face. Face. Face. Face. Face. Face. Face. Face.
Image. Image. Image. Image. Image. Image. Image.
Face. Face. Face. Face. Face. Face. Face. Face. Face. Face.
Image. Image. Image. Image. Image. Image. Image.
Face. Face. Face. Face. Face. Face. Face. Face. Face. Face.
Image. Image. Image. Image. Image. Image. Image.
Face. Face. Face. Face. Face. Face. Face. Face. Face. Face.

Any questions?

94. EDUCATION

We've gone over how whacked China is in terms of over-emphasis on rote studying, so anything having to do with learning how to add skills or get ahead…is growing. This is certainly not limited to students.

My prediction: the entire Self-Help industry is going to have a China field day; less on the books, because anything with IP will definitely be pirated, but more on the networking, face-giving, seminars.

95. CASH IN ON KIDS

This may be a surprise to you, but the kids in China are a lot like the kids *everywhere* else. They want to play and their parents' want them be healthy, study hard and then they can have fun. So pretty much anything that falls into one of the above opportunities is only going to get bigger here.

A special note really needs to be made about the Generation Gaps here. The pace of development of this country is absolutely staggering and the kids, especially in the cities, who were born after 1980 are SO VERY different from the previous generation. Teenage angst and the expression of it are, growing.

96. GOING GREEN

Green/Clean Technology is my personal favorite and something the country definitely needs.

On a macro level, China's central government is aware of the need and sees the benefits of going green. It also has in many ways, the ability to get things going more effectively than in the West.

On a micro level, to make the opportunities of going green work, underlying personal motivations need to be appealed to and when presented properly, it should not matter if, "good, greed, or face" are the triggers.

To make this work for consumers – "Going Green" needs to have a PR campaign in China led by popular pop stars. The people, for the most part, don't think about it too much until it affects them personally, in which case it's too late.

To make this work for you when dealing with the lower level government types – focus on the face-earning and profit potential. Any use of "guilt," you throw into the mix should be made as a side comment about what *other* people are saying. You?

You are here to make them a hero, and rich.

97. THE ANTI MARKET

I cannot finish this book without bringing up one very important option: NOT marketing to the Chinese at all.

You can simply make use of their low wages and use China as your manufacturing base while selling to other parts of the world.

Then, you don't need to worry about marketing campaigns, red tape or HR at all.

Section VIII

Odds & Ends / Closing Thoughts

98. GET THE DOUGH BEFORE YOU GO, THEN GROW SLOW

Do not go into China thinking you are going to strike it rich, fast. And do not go into China thinking you are going to spend pennies and make millions. In China, under-capitalization will put you out of business just like it will in the West and you will probably spend as much putting your business together as you will in the West (because of all the mistakes you will make).

Gather approximately twice as much capital as you think you'll need when you start putting your new China enterprise together. If you're representing a corporation, make sure you have plenty of supplies to get all the way through the desert before you leave the oasis – yes, meaning about twice what you think you'll need.

One distinct advantage of starting a business in China is your opportunity to capitalize on *China Fever* while you're courting investors. Everyone wants to be in on what's happening here now.

Go to people you know who have money and ask for three things:

1. Advice
2. Money
3. Connections

The introduction sounds something like this, "NAME, thanks for taking the time to discuss my project. Just to be clear, I'm here looking for (I would count out on my fingers) Advice on how to make this plan better, Capital to fund it and if you think it appropriate, Introductions to people who may be able to provide me with #1 and 2."

At the very least, you will walk away from each meeting with something and you'll certainly need them all.

When I look back at my Beijing Sammies experience, if I had it to do over again, I would have stayed smaller, longer. Beijing Sammies grew too fast. And in the end, not having the capital to weather the storm was our fatal flaw.

99. FRIENDS & OTHER EXOTIC CREATURES

A true friend is hard to find anywhere, but in China? Really tough.

Doing business in China, you'll meet plenty of people who care more about what you can do for them than about the intangible, emotional benefits of a strong personal connection. To them, a good friend is a *useful* friend – someone who brings money, face or Guanxi to the table. A lot of Westerners in China find this difficult to deal with.

This disconnect has a lot to do, I think, with profoundly different cultural paradigms about the role of friendship and how you know when a true friendship has been formed. Your average Westerner can be on close, intimate terms with someone fairly quickly, and even end up as good buddies after a few meetings.

Childhood friends aside, because you are not going to build any of those; beyond a certain age, Chinese rarely decide to be mates for life.

And let's be real: you are in China to get stuff done and the people with whom you come in contact are also looking to get stuff done. Don't forget, as strangers in a somewhat xenophobic culture, the fact that we are "foreigners" is also at work, creating a very real separation between you and them.

Rarely is hurt or rejection intended. Nevertheless, being sidelined by someone you thought of as a pal can hit you pretty hard the first few times you experience it. That being said, if you're an open, honest person with integrity (and an outgoing personality) you will form friendships in China. It'll probably just take some patience to find and develop them.

The way to build great friendships in China is to build them the way the Chinese do: see it as an investment. Use the superficial quality of most Chinese "friendships" to your advantage.

Haven't talked to _____ in a while but need a favor and know he's just the guy to do it? Pick up the phone and chat him up like no time has passed. Then, lay it on him (as long as it doesn't require a lot of his time or energy). And when he calls you a few months later and does the same thing, do your best to come through for him – as long as what he's asking is reasonable.

100. THE CHINA BUBBLE

No, I'm not talking about a real-estate bubble. I'm talking about a bubble that insulates quite a few expatriates and trailing spouses during their stay in China, a bubble that prevents them from ever actually experiencing anything remotely close to life in China.

You can recognize the bubble resident by the way, after a number of years, they still don't speak the language and possibly don't even care to learn it. They have their car and driver, two or three *ayis* (nannies/cleaning ladies) to do all their cooking, cleaning and laundry – and for those who have stayed long enough to have kids here - a lot of their child-rearing. They live in China, but they don't live *China*.

China is a tough place for most people, but for those who live in the China Bubble, it's soft – very, very soft. They're certainly very comfortable, even pampered and in fact, most of the bubble people couldn't live in China any other way. They can live the cushy lives they do because of the cheap labor market. I just wonder what the transition back into North American life is going to be like.

I know a number of people who see China as a temporary posting. I find it a shame to come to a country with SO MUCH to offer and then to keep it all at arm's length.

There are some really good people simply doing their "time" in China, but there are also the ones that give us the term "ugly foreigners." They complain all the time, tend to be loud and arrogant and the worst of them look down on the Chinese. They should do everyone a big favor and just go home.

Unfortunately, you can find them all over the place. Shanghai is rabid with them. Beijing runs a close second. The good news is, the farther you get from the first-tier cities, the fewer you'll encounter. (This is *especially* good news for *you*, because you're going second-tier, right?) Life is just too tough for them anywhere else on the mainland.

If you have a small business, don't hire them. They're poison. Don't hang out with them. They'll bring you down; both emotionally and through guilt by association.) And please, whatever you do, don't become one!

101. THE PACE OF THE RACE

Hmmm... how do I describe the unique pace of China?

On the micro level, the deal making, is slow, slow, slow. When it comes to individual enterprises, Chinese deal-makers *talk* momentum, but actually progress at a snail's pace. They want to make sure they can trust you and that you have a strong relationship in place before they move forward. Instead of "Ready, aim, fire!" the thoughtful Chinese approach tends to be "Ready, aim, aim more precisely, aim even *more* precisely, fire!"

At the same time, they'll usually expect and rely on rapid responses from your end. Through experiences dealing with Western firms, most Chinese have learned to plan and strategize with our taste for acceleration in mind. But almost always, there's another agenda at work, at the very same time. By being as "slow-as-molasses" themselves but expecting you to respond and produce results in a heartbeat they can keep you unsettled and therefore more vulnerable.

For most Chinese, keeping the upper hand (even once a good working relationship is in place and humming along) is not only desirable, it's a conscious goal.

What does this mean for you? You will hurry up and wait – a lot. So, you'll need to approach deals with that understanding. Double your projected timelines, at a

minimum. Triple them to be safe. And don't make deadline promises to your partners, your boss or yourself that you won't be able to keep. In short, try not to make promises when it comes to timing at all.

You will have to guard against a tendency to become their bitch, when it comes to scheduling and milestones. Meaning: you'll have to approach project progression as an aspect of negotiation, being careful not to apologize for failing to read the 300-page report they gave you last night at 5:00 p.m. by 9:00 a.m. this morning.

And you will have an outstanding opportunity to develop your patience muscles.

The macro level is a whole other story.

The Chinese economy itself is moving at lightning speed. Foreigners and Chinese alike who leave for a year or two hardly recognize the place when they return, because so much has changed and developed. The growth is actually discernible every day, like summer grass that grows faster than you can mow it.

This means you will literally run a different business on Friday than you ran on Thursday.

Here's the "pace of the race" rule of thumb:

- When it comes to individual deals, the pace can be grindingly slow.

- When it comes to China business as a whole, hold on to your hat!

102. TWINKIES™, BANANAS & HARD BOILED EGGS

Bananas are good for you; Twinkies, not so much.

You know what I'm talking about, people of Chinese ancestry who come to China from the West, yellow on the outside, but white on the inside. They fall into two distinct groups.

Bananas are made up of those seeking to re-connect with their roots and/or find themselves. They come back to China to actually study the language, immerse themselves in the culture and become more "Chinese."

They've usually grown up with many traditional (even antiquated) Chinese customs. So, they have an understanding of and connection with China that even foreigners living in China for many years may never have. They long to be immersed and absorbed into China's culture. When they first arrive, they are completely out of touch with modern China and are blown away by the difference between their romantic notions and the rushing, post-Communist reality of modern China.

Twinkies are composed of cocky, arrogant types who feel they have an inside scoop on China, simply by virtue of their genes.

The arrogance of Twinkies grates on the locals even more than the naiveté of the bananas. Twinkies don't get the subtle nuances that only come with growing up here. But they're not willing to cop to it.

Both Twinkies and Bananas can get chewed up and spit out fairly quickly – there's not a lot of love or tolerance for them. Neither group gets the slack Caucasian Westerners get. The (white) foreigner is forgiven for being an ignoramus and expected to stumble often and hilariously (because how could he or she possibly know?)

Unfortunately, Bananas are quite often resented for not knowing how to behave. Mistakes are felt more sharply because they look Chinese but have been spared the struggles and singular experiences of really *being* Chinese.

Then there is an odd bunch; the Hard Boiled Eggs: white on the outside and yellow on the inside… This bunch has been in China… too long. Yeah…

They tend to stay away from first-tier cities and foreigners in general, dress like 1960s China and only speak Chinese. If you see one, be sure to ask to take a picture with them. They love that.

103. KEEP IT TOGETHER

AKA Before you *really* lose your cool

You are going to have bad days. In fact here, you are going have bad *China* days. When you're enduring the latest form of Chinese water torture, it's easy to lose sight of all the positive experiences you're having, all the progress you're actually making... and it's really easy to look for someone to blame. It gets really easy to focus all your negative energy to the people around you, i.e., the Chinese.

Most Western nations are ethnically diverse. This means we have less temptation to generalize from a few negative experiences with one or two people who happen to be members of a specific ethnic group, to that group as a whole.

But in China, just about everyone you hire, bargain with or buy from will be Chinese. So, when things get rough and stay that way for awhile, you may find yourself feeling frustrated with **all** Chinese people – or even thinking thoughts like "Chinese people are so frickin' (enter negative comment here)!"

When you realize this is happening, you need to take a step back. (Before you really screw things up) Close your eyes, take a deep breath and count "10, 9, 8, 7..."

Take a break. Go for a walk, a workout, take a nap, a sick day, a long weekend, a vacation… whatever.

Just chill out.

When you calm down, don't beat yourself up. Recognize it for what it is: an urge to create a scapegoat. (One of our uglier human failings in times of stress, but one you can refuse to indulge in.)

Then, get your head screwed on straight, smile at the next person you see, and get back to the business of being a human being in the midst of other human beings.

Now go back and re-read the Chinese Water Torture and Chinese Fire Drill Chapters.

A piece of advice that has served me well for every time you see something in China that makes you go, "Are you ^%$@ KIDDING ME??!!!": You should be *thankful* that things are the way they are, because if everything was perfect, there would be no opportunity for you here.

104. TRUST SHOULD HAVE NOTHING TO DO WITH IT

Separate any partners and employees whose loyalty you're not 100% sure you possess from as much of your business's decision-making and spending power as possible. If you have a partner, make sure you and your people are the ones actually in charge of the hiring and firing. You want your true allies, the people you trust, overseeing the purchasing and financial management.

But no matter how much you might trust either or both of them, your accountant and your cashier can never be one and the same person, and here's why. In China, you don't always have to have a signature to get money from a bank. All you need is a chop, a seal that represents you. It's transportable, therefore dangerous. If someone has your chop, they have access to any accounts associated with it and can transfer or withdraw money in your account as they choose - so long as they have also have the bank book.

Kickbacks are a fact of life in China. So is embezzlement. If your purchaser is not loyal to you, there's a good chance they will be on the take. If the worst happens and you catch your purchaser with their hand in the cookie jar, nail them to the wall. Be swift. Be merciless. You've got to send out a zero-tolerance message loud and clear.

A successful Beijing restaurant went under because the management failed to operate according to this principle. Their accountant used their chop to embezzle the equivalent of $250,000 American dollars and cooked the books to cover it up. The restaurant's owner was not a native Chinese, but an American-born (and reared) son of Chinese parents. He lost his business because he did not keep his chop and bank book separated, each (or at least one!) in the hands of loyal people.

DEFINITELY STILL HALF FULL

Congratulations. You made it the whole way through.

Tenacity is something you will certainly need to survive and prosper in China. If you have any questions or if I forgot to put something in here, you can find new information on my blog www.where-east-eats-west.com.

I hope you have been educated and entertained.

If I scared you off well… consider yourself lucky.

I absolutely hope I have not turned you off China. This place is amazing, exciting and *the* place to be in our life time. As tough as it may be and after all I have been through, I still maintain a "glass half full" perspective.

And I hope you do too.

Be good.
Be safe,

Sam

Appendix A - My China Street Cred

September 1, 1995   **China Virgin**
Arrived in Beijing with zero Chinese language skills and not knowing a soul.

1997-2003   **Entrepreneur**   7 years
Founded and grew Beijing Sammies into a recognized brand name chain with 4 locations, a corporate catering business, online ordering, a centralized production facility, over 90 staff, annual revenues of $1M and systemized the company for franchising.

2003-2004   **Investment Consultant**   6 months
Consulted for six month for a Canadian investment company looking into a bringing a building system to China. Got as far into the dirty construction/real estate industry as necessary to convince the friendly, Canadian investment company to stay out of China and save their money.

2004-2006   **Executive Recruiter**   2 years
Client Partner for two years at the world's largest executive recruitment firm Korn/Ferry International (Beijing); earned a 95% closure rate.

2006-2007   **Westinghouse Consultant** 1.5 years
Consulted and negotiated for Westinghouse Nuclear throughout their bidding and winning of their $5.4

billion four nuclear power plant China project. Helped establish their China team, then left to get back to my entrepreneur self.

2007- 2009   IT Entrepreneur

Founded www.Me-2-B. Think EBay for hired services. The premise was people should be recognized and rewarded based on their proven ability to Get Stuff Done. When the economic crisis hit we shelved the project and gave the platform to an NGO.

2009- 2010   COO Climate Action & Author

Was brought on to build a team and design a platform to help 'green' China, by connecting Chinese people to green Chinese projects. The site was up and running in 6 months but when the CEO decided to focus on selling carbon credits, we left.

2010- Present Co founder 非常好看.com

www.feichanghaokan.com

FCHK is a contest-based social media promotional platform that allows brands to engage consumers in exchange for prizes and opportunities. FCHK shall be China's first internet brand that goes global.

Since 1999, I've given lectures on entrepreneurship, the challenges associated to the China Market, H.R. in China and starting a business in China, to various MBA courses, Pricewaterhouse, MIT and international schools (in both English and Chinese).

Index

*Note: Some areas in the index are implied and not exactly corresponding.

Trust, 49, 106, 117, 128, 153, 207, 247, 253
Twinkies, 249

U

Undercover Entrepreneurs, 157
University of Western Ontario (UWO), 21

Upper Canada College, 20

W

Widgets, 38
World Famous Brands, 96
Wrestling, 19, 21, 22